A Travel ✶ Guide to

COLONIAL
BOSTON

Other books in the Travel Guide series:

A Travel ✦ Guide to

COLONIAL BOSTON

By James Barter

LUCENT
BOOKS®

THOMSON
———✦———™
GALE

San Diego • Detroit • New York • San Francisco • Cleveland • New Haven, Conn. • Waterville, Maine • London • Munich

LIBRARY OF CONGRESS CATALOGING-IN-PUBLICATION DATA

Barter, James, 1946–
    Colonial Boston / by James Barter.
        p. cm. — (A travel guide to:)
Summary: A visitor's guide to the weather, historic sights, food, shopping, and
overnight accommodations of Colonial Boston.
Includes bibliographical references and index.
    ISBN 1-59018-357-6 (alk. paper)
    1. Boston (Mass.)—History—Colonial period, ca. 1600–1775—Juvenile literature.
2. Boston (Mass.)—Social life and customs—Juvenile literature. 3. Boston (Mass.)—
Guidebooks—Juvenile literature. [1. Boston (Mass.)—History—Colonial period,
ca. 1600–1775. 2. Boston (Mass.)—Social life and customs. 3. Boston (Mass.)—
Description and travel.] I. title. II. Travel guide (Lucent Books).
    F73.4.B37 2004
    974.4'6102—dc22
                                                                    2003011840

Printed in the United States of America

Contents

Foreword

Travel can be a unique way to learn about oneself and other cultures. The esteemed American writer and historian, John Hope Franklin, poetically expressed his conviction in the value of travel by urging, "We must go beyond textbooks, go out into the bypaths and untrodden depths of the wilderness and travel and explore and tell the world the glories of our journey." The message communicated by this eloquent entreaty is clear: The value of travel is to temper one's imagination about a place and its people with reality, and instead of thinking how things may be, to be able to experience them as they really are.

Franklin's voice is not alone in his summons for students to "travel and explore." He is joined by a stentorian chorus of thinkers that includes former president John F. Kennedy, who established the Peace Corps to facilitate cross-cultural understandings between Americans and citizens of other lands. Ideas about the benefits of travel do not spring only from contemporary times. The ancient Greek historian Herodotus journeyed to foreign lands for the purpose of immersing himself in unfamiliar cultural traditions. In this way, he believed, he might gain a first-hand understanding of people and ways of life in other places.

The joys, insights, and satisfaction that travelers derive from their journeys are not limited to cultural understanding. Travel has the added value of enhancing the traveler's inner self by expanding his or her range of experiences. Writer Paul Tournier concurs that, "The real meaning of travel, like that of a conversation by the fireside, is the discovery of oneself through contact with other people."

The Lucent Books Travel Guide series enlivens history by introducing a new and innovative style and format. Each volume in the series presents the history of a preeminent historical travel destination written in the casual style and format of a travel guide. Whether providing a tour of fifth-century B.C. Athens, Renaissance Florence, or Shakespeare's London, each book describes a city or area at its cultural peak and orients readers to only those places and activities that are known to have existed at that time.

A high level of authenticity is achieved in the Travel Guide series. Each book is written in the present tense and addresses the reader as a prospective foreign traveler. The sense of authenticity is further achieved, whenever possible, by the inclusion of descriptive quotations by contemporary writers who knew the place; information on fascinating historical sites; and travel tips meant to explain unusual cultural idiosyncrasies that give depth and texture to all great cultural centers. Even shopping details, such as where to buy an ermine-trimmed gown, or a much-needed house slave, are included to inform readers of what items were sought after throughout history.

Looked at collectively, this series presents an appealing presentation of many of the cultural and social highlights of Western civilization. The collection also provides a framework for discussion about the larger historical currents that dominated not only each travel destination but countries and entire continents as well. Each book is customized by the author to bring to the fore the most important and most interesting characteristics that define each title. High standards of scholarship are assured in the series by the generous peppering of relevant quotes and extensive bibliographies. These tools provide readers a scholastic standard for their own research as well as a guide to direct them to other books, periodicals, and websites that will provide them greater breadth and detail.

Freedom's Birthplace

Ten years ago, in 1783, the War of Independence officially ended with the signing of the Treaty of Paris. Today, all of Boston is preparing for the tenth anniversary that will be celebrated on the Fourth of July to coincide with the signing of the Declaration of Independence. This year's festivities promise to be more spectacular, more patriotic, more dazzling than ever before, and on a far grander scale than those being planned elsewhere—even more spectacular than in New York and Philadelphia. After all, Boston is the city where it all began; it is the birthplace of American freedom.

Boston's prominence, which will be celebrated in the upcoming festivities, is not the result of good fortune but rather the result of a history of strong conviction. Boston's history is different from that of other cities because it speaks of remarkable persistence in the pursuit of freedom. Founded by Puritans more than

160 years ago, Reverend Richard Baxter urged his religious followers to commit themselves to work toward freedom and to perform good works for Boston's community. He said, "As soon as you are capable of performance, the vow is upon yourselves to do it."[1] With these inspirational words and the commitment to hard work by his congregation, our Puritan forefathers set to the task of building a beautiful, new city while nourishing many freedoms denied them in England.

This same spirit was called upon again just twenty years ago when Bostonians recognized that their need for freedom was in conflict with the English Crown, which denied them lives as free men and women. This collision of wills summoned the passions of great Bostonians such as John and Samuel Adams, who ardently and publicly spoke out against the tyranny of the English. These great orators were joined by Benjamin Franklin and John Hancock, who wrote treatises in support of overthrowing English rule and dared to place their signatures on the Declaration of Independence. Joining as well were Paul Revere and William Dawes, who mounted their horses the night of April 18, 1775, and rode throughout the Boston countryside warning patriots to take up arms and assemble for war at Lexington and Concord.

So strong was the resolve of Boston's Sons of Liberty at that historical juncture

Paul Revere warns Bostonians that British troops are preparing an attack. Revere and other local patriots were instrumental to the success of the American Revolution.

that the English general Thomas Gage said of these and other Boston patriots, "These people show a spirit and conduct against us they never showed against the French. They are now spirited up by a rage and enthusiasm as great as ever people were possessed of."[2]

The spirit of freedom carries on today. The past ten years of peace have been a time to bind the city's war wounds with new public buildings. Boston's new wharf, for example, is capable of accommodating dozens of great triple- and quadruple-masted clipper ships from exotic ports as

Bostonians gather at the State House to hear a reading of the Declaration of Independence.

Boston's skyline in 1774. Since the end of the Revolution, the city has blossomed into a vibrant cultural center that welcomes ships and visitors from all over the world.

far away as the West Indies, Europe, and even Cathay [China]. These ships provide the citizens of Boston with the freshest of foods, the finest quality home furnishings, and the latest fashions. The people of Boston continue to promote education by building some of America's finest schools that graduate architects and engineers. These graduates have constructed a lively downtown area near the docks as well as parks and promenades pleasing to all who enjoy strolling the modern streets.

Ben Franklin, publisher.

Slowly Boston is emerging as the crown jewel of the new American republic. The city is more beautiful than ever, and it is at the vanguard of the fledgling nation as the commercial, social, and cultural center of America. This Fourth of July, thousands will flock here to visit and experience the many places where the revolution began. Come visit the historic buildings where the words of patriotic orators stirred Boston's minutemen to action and to acts of civil disobedience that enraged the oppressive English. The city has never been a better travel destination for sightseers, and it has already established itself as the nation's greatest out-of-doors museum celebrating the nation's birth.

11

Chapter 1

A City on a Hill: A Brief History of Boston

Some old-timers say that Indian tribes occupied Boston and its environs seven thousand years ago. They further claim, and most locals say it is so, that it was not until one thousand years ago that the Massachusetts tribe, one of several that were a part of the greater Algonquin Indian nation, settled here. The name Massachusetts is an Algonquian word meaning "near the great hill," a reference to the three hills that stand shoulder-to-shoulder in the Tramount district overlooking the city.

The Massachusetts tribe at one time numbered three thousand and lived in several well-organized communities. Like most other tribes along the New England seaboard, the Massachusetts Indians were farmers of the land and fishers of the water. They grew a small variety of vegetables, raised fields of corn, fished the Charles and Mystic Rivers, and harvested shellfish and lobster from the saltwater harbor. During the harsh winters, however, the Massachusetts hunkered down in their wigwams and survived by hunting and trapping animals, and eating dried fruits and stored nuts.

By the time the first English arrived, the number of Massachusetts Indians had declined to about one thousand scattered throughout twenty villages. The reason for their declining numbers is not known with certainty, but many locals who still sometimes trade with them claim that it may have been a combination of disease and poor hunting.

The Arrival of the Puritans

Two hundred years ago the first European explorers began to tentatively inch their way down the New England coastline, stopping at Indian villages such as those in Boston. Spurred on by dreams of great wealth, explorers searched for natural resources such as gold, furs for fashionable coats and hats, and stocks of lumber and large fish, all of which could be shipped back home to Europe. Explorers had visited the Boston area many times but it was not until 1614 that John Smith mapped the Boston Bay and declared it a paradise, that greater interest was triggered in the region.

Not all explorers of New England's coastline were looking for riches. One such group from England was a group called the Puritans. This Christian sect was in search of a new home for its followers whose rigorous adherence to the teachings of the Bible was in conflict with that of the Church of England. One of the Puritan leaders, John Winthrop, negotiated with King Charles II to establish a Puritan township called the Massachusetts Bay Colony. In April 1630, the first group of Puritans departed Plymouth, England, for their new home in Boston. Jammed into seventeen small rickety ships, more than one thousand Puritans set sail. Winthrop wrote of their reluctance to travel home in his journal: "We cannot part from our native country without much sadness of heart and many tears in our eyes."[3]

The first group of Puritans pushes off from an English beach in search of a new home in America.

After two hellish months of relentless high seas and deep swells, the hardy survivors were rewarded with their first sighting of Boston. The Shawmut Peninsula, a small spit of land jutting between the Atlantic Ocean to the east and the freshwater bay to the west, first attracted the Puritans to the area. Created by the outfall of the Charles and Mystic Rivers on the west, the Shawmut proved to be an advantageously situated site for a city. Realizing the strategic and economic importance of a piece of land that is protected on three sides by water, Winthrop and his followers built simple homes at the base of Beacon Hill, the tallest hill on the peninsula, making this area Boston's first residential neighborhood.

Growth and Prosperity

As the seventeenth century pushed forward, ample prosperity blessed the colonists. Within ten years, the population of Boston doubled to two thousand and by 1675 it doubled again. As the city grew, homes and businesses spread north and south of Beacon Hill and all along the east side where the wharf grew to accommodate a flurry of trade. The dozens

Puritans arrive on Boston's Shawmut Peninsula. These early settlers constructed the city's first neighborhood at the base of Beacon Hill.

Tough Times at Lost Town

When the Puritans arrived in 1630 to set up their religious enclave, Boston was nothing more than a hilly, treeless peninsula covered by blueberry bushes and surrounded by rank-smelling mudflats and briny shallows. According to eyewitness accounts, the region was virtually hidden from visitors who arrived by sea. The many nearby islands blocked the view of ships as they approached the Shawmut Peninsula. Dubbed "Lost Town" by the sailors who threaded their ships through the many islands, few were initially able to see many virtues for settling here.

The earliest houses that huddled along the coast were made with thatched roofs and walls of wattle and daub (straw mixed with mud that hardens to make simple walls). Wood was a scarce resource because to get it the colonists had to row their boats to islands where a few sparse trees were cut and brought back to the city on their flat keel boats.

Whenever a large merchant ship snaked its way into the harbor, the excitement quickly spread down the dirt streets, attracting rich and poor to hurry down to the dock to see who had arrived, to learn what news the passengers brought from other towns, and to trade what few things they could harvest or make in exchange for the desperately needed provisions the boat delivered.

The toughest struggle for the settlers of Lost Town was surviving the first few severe winters. The tough times were highlighted by an entry in the journal of John Winthrop on January 13, 1638. This writing recounts part of a story about thirty men who set out to the nearby Spectacle Island to gather wood, as quoted in Carl Seaburg's book, *Boston Observed*: "Three of them gate [got] home the next day over the ice, but their hands and feet frozen. Some lost their fingers, and one died. The rest went from Spectacle Island to the main, but two of them fell into the ice."

of docks were littered with crates of food, tea, clothing, lumber, iron, exotic skins and furs, colorful silks and delicate porcelain for well-to-do Boston families, aromatic herbs and spices, household goods, and even pet monkeys. Shipping and sea-related commerce employed a majority of the workers. At this still early stage in the city's short history, Bostonians were in control of their destiny. At New England's busiest harbor, dozens of three- and four-masted freighters from England, Spain, France, Portugal, New York, and Phila-

delphia poured into the harbor on a daily basis.

Boston's wharf was awash in the shouts of captains docking their ships, the colors of exotic merchandise, the smells of foods from around the world, and the pushing and shoving of broad-shouldered dock workers.

The economic backbone of the city was shipping, and this was made evident by the dense population along the wharves from the north to south ends of the city. In addition to the handling of thousands of tons of cargo, hundreds of shops supporting the population of the city also spread from the water's edge inland as far back as Cornhill, Hanover, Middle, and North Streets.

Flushed with a sense of limitless financial and spiritual potential, Bostonians foresaw no restrictions to their future success in their city that Winthrop characterized as "a city on a hill, a shinning beacon that would attract the eyes of all people."[4] As enthusiasm for commerce soared, one of those sets of eyes—those of the king of England—fixed a covetous stare on the American colonies, seeing an opportunity to get rich on the hardworking backs of Bostonians.

The Road to Revolution

The Bostonian spirit soared despite the sobering reality that the city's future remained firmly within the grip of King Charles II. A variety of English laws gov-

During the seventeenth century, Boston was home to the busiest harbor in the American colonies.

Colonists burn stamps to protest the Stamp Act.

erning trade and navigation became increasingly restrictive, preventing merchants from shipping their products to countries other than England and stipulating that all goods produced in Boston were to be more tightly controlled by English merchants and shippers. In 1660 England passed additional laws that restricted what merchandise and natural resources Boston colonists could export and forbade any European countries from directly shipping goods to the colonies.

By 1700 these repressive trade laws, which stole from the pockets of merchants and lined the coffers of the king, did not sit well with the leading merchants of Boston. The tense situation worsened when King George imposed yet more taxes aimed directly at all colonial trading cities. Known as the Sugar Act, the Stamp Act, and the Townshend Acts, these taxes placed additional financial burdens on colonists, covering a broad array of goods and permits needed for a variety of activities, from owning shops and printing newspapers to getting married.

Bostonians responded with outcries of "foul play," and in time, they came up with what would become the hallmark cry of the revolution: "no taxation without representation." They also responded to the unjust taxes by agreeing not to purchase any English goods until the Stamp Act was repealed. To confront this repression, a few Bostonians dared step to the fore, organizing opposition to the hated English king.

Acts of Civil Disobedience

Boston leaders now understood that their desire for freedom and the king's need to control the colonies were incompatible goals. Motivated by the fiery rhetoric of

Colonial Boston

Bostonian John Adams, citizens began to organize resistance at secretly held meetings in local taverns. In his diary Adams noted that patriotic meetings "tinge [touch] the Minds of the People, they impregnate them with the sentiments of Liberty. They render the People fond of their Leaders in the Cause, and averse and bitter against all opposers."[5]

Citizens took to the streets and wharves in protest of England's heavy-handed taxes. They dumped over carts filled with English goods and roughed up English custom officers. They hurled stones and vegetables at the homes of English officials and any Bostonians viewed as supporters of the English. When English officials seized the sloop *Liberty*, belonging to John Hancock, in Boston Harbor in 1768, the Sons of Liberty stormed down to the customs office and threatened violence if the sloop was not released.

By 1769 minor violence and verbal harassment prompted the English to station four thousand troops in Boston. With a population of fifteen thousand, Bostonians felt smothered by such a large force, derisively calling them *redcoats* because of their bright red uniforms. Redcoats who manned checkpoints detained and interrogated citizens while occupying the Boston Common, the city's largest open space, and using it as a parade ground and camp. Bostonians were further infuriated when forced to house many of the troops and tolerate their coarse remarks. Some patriots even lost their jobs to redcoats in need of extra money.

British ships arrive in Boston Harbor to seize the Liberty. *Such action angered Bostonians and spurred them to rebel against English rule.*

redcoats spilled out of an adjacent customhouse, leveled their muskets on the unruly crowd, and fired, killing five and wounding eight. The Boston newspaper the *Gazette* labeled the incident a bloody massacre.

For the next three years, relations between Bostonians and English troops continued to smolder until November 1773, when words of anger escalated to acts of violence. Outraged by the tea tax, Bostonians who got word of three English tea ships in the harbor warned dock workers not to unload the tea chests. On the night of December 16, a handful of gutsy citizens dressed as Indians stormed down to the wharf where the tea ships were tied up. In the cover of night, chests of tea were chopped open and dumped into the harbor. John Adams wrote of this act:

Angry Bostonians tear down a statue of England's King George.

Boston was a powder keg ready to explode. The eruption came on a cold snowy day, March 5, 1770, when a crowd of Boston rope workers assaulted some redcoats with hard-packed snowballs and chunks of ice on King Street. As the alarm bells of the Brick Church rang out,

This is the most significant Moment of all. This destruction of the tea is so bold, so daring, so firm, intrepid, and inflexible, and it must have important Consequences and so lasting, that I cannot but consider it as an Epoch in history.[6]

This success emboldened more acts of insurrection. In 1774 representatives of

The Tea Party

Sightseers who come to Boston to learn about the role the city played in the revolution will find many historic places where the Boston Tea Party was planned and executed. Since this was one of the great demonstrations of civil disobedience that led up to the war, its history is recommended reading before taking your trip.

On May 10, 1773, the English authorized the East India Co. to export one-half million pounds of tea to the American colonies. At the same time, they imposed a new tax on tea drinkers. It is not surprising that this new tax, which followed many other unfair taxes on sugar, stamps, and a variety of everyday commodities, became the last straw.

On November 27, 1773, three ships loaded with tea from the East India Co. landed at Boston but were prevented from unloading their cargo. Demanding that the tea be returned to where it came from or face retribution, the Sons of Liberty, led by Samuel Adams, began to develop a strategy for ridding Boston of the cargo onboard the three ships.

On the evening of December 16, 1773, a large band of patriots disguised as Mohawk Indians burst from the Old South Meeting House and headed toward the three ships at Griffin's Wharf. Quickly and in an orderly manner, the patriots boarded each of the tea ships and went to work breaking open the airtight tea chests with axes and hatchets while two thousand spectators watched from the wharf. Once the crates were opened, the patriots dumped the tea into the sea. By nine o'clock, the Sons of Liberty had emptied a total of 342 crates of tea into Boston Harbor. They then swept the ships' decks and made each ship's first mate sign an affidavit attesting that only the tea was damaged.

When the "tea party" was over, the patriots and the spectators marched past the home of English admiral Montague, making a second statement of contempt for English rule. According to the Boston Tea Party Ship and Museum, Montague came to his front porch and yelled to the crowd as it passed, "Well boys, you have had a fine pleasant evening for your Indian caper, haven't you? But mind, you have got to pay the fiddler yet!"

Colonists dressed as Mohawk Indians empty crates of tea into Boston Harbor.

all colonies hurried to Philadelphia to form the Continental Congress with the objective of declaring independence from England. John Adams, his cousin Samuel Adams, and Paul Revere represented Boston. On April 18, 1775, to counter this act of rebellion, English general Thomas Gage ordered his troops to cross the Charles River, march the remainder of the twenty miles from Boston to the nearby towns of Concord and Lexington, and to destroy hidden caches of ammunitions. Paul Revere and William Dawes, who got wind of this action, rode throughout the countryside urging the local militia—also known as the minutemen because each was ready for war at a minute's notice— to hurry to Concord and Lexington with loaded muskets. At the same time, Robert Newman climbed the steeple at the North Church and suspended two lanterns. For all who knew this secret code, it warned that the English were advancing up the Charles River.

The Revolutionary War and Boston

The minutemen drew the battle line at Concord Bridge. As General Gage and his troops approached the old bridge and

General Gage.

ordered the minutemen to stand aside, the militia took aim at the English line of musketeers. No one knows who fired first, but by the end of the day, 93 patriots lay dead or badly wounded. The English lost 272 men. The War of Independence was on.

Raging against the au-

Signal from North Church.

dacious actions of the minutemen, Gage began a siege of Boston. Thousands of minutemen hurried to Boston and occupied Breed and Bunker Hills in Charles Town, immediately across the channel at the north end of the city. On June 17, 1775, both armies began an artillery bombardment that killed 230 English and wounded 800. Minutemen losses were half what the English suffered. Badly mauled, Gage's army broke off the battle and pulled back to the Boston Common where they stayed for the duration of the year.

During the long winter, Gage's troops consumed most of Boston's food, pulled down more than one hundred buildings, and ripped out the pews from Old South Meeting Hall for firewood. They even pulled down and burned the steeple of North Church. The siege finally ended in early March 1776 when Boston bookseller Henry Knox and George Washington, General of the Continental army, occupied Dorchester Heights with cannons and drove the redcoats from the city.

On March 17 the English evacuated the city and on July 18 Bostonians gathered at the State House to hear the first reading of the Declaration of Independence. Nonetheless, the destruction by the redcoats was devastating and prompted an anonymous patriot to pen this depressing description of the city:

It presented an indescribable scene of desolation and gloominess, for notwithstanding the joyous occasion of having driven our enemies from our land, our minds were impressed with an awful sadness at the sight of the

Patriots fight British soldiers outside Boston. The first battles at Lexington and Concord were victories for the colonists.

General George Washington takes command of the Continental Army. Washington and his army drove the British out of Boston in March 1776.

ruins of so many houses which had been taken down for fuel—the dirtiness of the streets—the wretched appearance of the very few inhabitants who remained during the siege.[7]

Gage and war never returned to Boston and the War of Independence finally ended in 1783. Peace had come but the city was in a state of disarray and destruction. However, just ten years later, church steeples have been repaired, houses rebuilt, and the wharf is busier than ever. Far from being dependent on the English for prosperity, Boston has never been more enjoyable. This summer's festivities celebrating independence will be a great time to visit and learn more about the city's history.

Chapter 2

Arrival, Weather, and Location

B oston is a city with the sea as its front door and a rhythm of life that revolves around its salt-sprayed harbor. Boston's waterfront, down along the eastside wharf, remains the heart and soul of the burgeoning cosmopolitan city. Visitors immediately recognize that it is the center of activity and the place that everyone, directly or indirectly, depends on for their livelihood, social position, and the simple joys of life.

One of the joys of the docks is their unmistakable and pleasurable smells. At any time, on any day, Bostonians and visitors stroll the docks, look with astonishment at more than one hundred seagoing ships, and take in the exotic aromas of coffee beans from the West Indies, chests of teas originating in India and Cathay, and sacks of aromatic spices.

Another simple joy of the waterfront is its lively, colorful, and noisy excitement. As great sailing ships tie up to one of the city's dozens of docks, workers heave chests of tea and silk from the holds of China clipper ships, roll out monstrous bales of cotton and tobacco from southern American states, and winch tons of sugar from the West Indies in great nets onto the wharves. Along the smaller docks, away from the center of commerce, carts filled with local fish and live lobster crackle over the noisy cobblestone streets en route to fish markets throughout the city.

Weather in Boston

Without a doubt, the best time to visit America's birthplace is during the annual Independence Day celebration on the Fourth of July. The festive occasion falls right in the middle of the best season to visit the city: from May through October, with late spring and early autumn the most pleasant of all. The sea breeze keeps Boston cooler in summer (in the low seventies) and somewhat

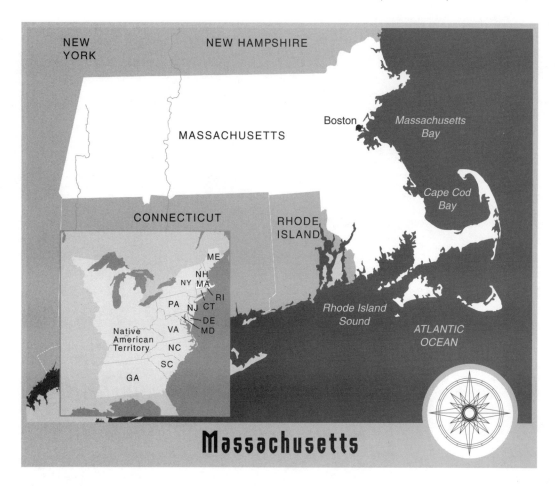

NEW YORK

NEW HAMPSHIRE

MASSACHUSETTS

Boston

Massachusetts Bay

Cape Cod Bay

CONNECTICUT

RHODE ISLAND

Rhode Island Sound

ATLANTIC OCEAN

ME

NH
MA
NY
RI
PA
NJ CT
DE
VA MD
Native American Territory
NC
SC
GA

Massachusetts

more moderate than its northern latitude might indicate in winter. Unseasonably hot or cold weather may occur at any time. This presents the city with summers that are milder than what sightseers from New York and Philadelphia might expect but with colder winters. Winters, in fact, are best to avoid, especially if visits are planned by boat because from time to time the entire harbor freezes over, preventing boats from entering and keeping those already tied up at the wharf from departing.

In a word, Boston's weather is changeable; you can expect alternating sun and precipitation all year. The ocean's proximity also means that Boston has fairly high humidity levels, which can make summer heat sticky and winter winds biting.

Arriving by Boat

If your visit to the city involves sailing either from Europe or from northern or southern ports along the Atlantic seaboard, it is best to use one of the larger

Booking passage on a large commercial schooner like this one or on a smaller vessel that sails with a group is the safest way to travel to Boston by sea.

commercial schooners or to book passage on one of the smaller vessels that travel in groups. Although sea lanes far out to sea are safe, pirate activity closer to the shoreline shoals continues to prove problematic to vulnerable ships. More than one passenger ship has mounted what appear from a distance to be cannons but are in reality wood replicas painted black to fool pirates into keeping their distance. Such cannons are lightheartedly called "Quaker cannons" in quirky reference to the pacifism practiced by members of the Quaker church.

Very often one nation's pirates are another nation's privateers. Privateers are ships that carry legal sanctions to raid enemy vessels. Such international efforts, most notably between Spain, England, and France, pose some threat to ships arriving from Europe. When pirates are caught, they are strung up on a gallows displayed on the mudflats on the south end for all to see. This poem describes the hanging of six pirates:

> Ye pirates who against God's law
> did fight.
> Have all been taken which is right.
> Some of them were old and others
> young,
> And on the flats of Boston they were
> hung.[8]

The U.S. government is in the process of building a fleet of warships to end the scourge of piracy. Just this year, President George Washington authorized the construction of six frigates to protect the coastline, the largest of which will be built and homeported in Boston and will be christened the USS *Constitution*.

First Glimpse of the City

If your arrival will be by boat from England or France, expect your trip to take between eighteen and twenty-one days, depending on the winds and currents. You will have your first glimpse of Boston Harbor about thirty miles out to sea and to the north as your boat skirts

Blackbeard the pirate.

the coastline passing close to Cape Ann. The sighting of Cape Ann signals the end of the voyage. At this point, the captain will begin a slow right turn toward the city.

As boats approach within five miles of the city, they drop sails to negotiate the maze of small islands with names such as Deer, Apple, Hog, and Bumpkin. In the event that ship arrivals coincide with darkness or dense fog, Boston Lighthouse, which towers seventy-five feet above the surf on Brewster Island, safely guides boats into the harbor. This conical stone tower has several whale-oil lamps lit by the lighthouse keepers who have acquired the nickname of "wickies" because they trim and light the wicks that burn the whale-oil fuel.

Threading their way around the southern tip of Noodle Island, passengers get their first glimpse of Boston as it comes into full view. At this moment of excitement, take the opportunity to stand on the ship's prow for a full panoramic view of Boston—this will be your only chance to experience this unique view. Dead ahead the entire expanse of the city stretches before the boat as it

The Shawmut Peninsula

First-time travelers arriving by boat will soon see that the city, which deceptively has the look of an island, actually occupies all of the Shawmut Peninsula. Shawmut has a highly irregular spiderlike coastline characterized by indented coves that alternate with jagged jetties. It is this highly irregular coastline that provides ample safe anchorages for ships. At the same time, the peninsula, which extends out into the bay, provides security for the city against possible intruders.

Dead in the middle of the east side, entering boats head into the Great Cove, the major wharf area of the peninsula, immediately behind which is the city's most prominent landmark, Tramount Hill. This hill, which is actually a short ridge of three hills, provides Bostonians with an ideal lookout spot. Beacon Hill, the middle and tallest of the three hills, is named as such due to its fire beacon, which can be set on fire to signal all Bostonians of approaching danger. According to Andrew Buni and Alan Rogers, in their book titled the Massachusetts Bay Company declared in 1634 that "there shall be a beacon set on the highest hill in Boston to give notice to the country of any danger."

The most northern tip of the city, locally known as the North End, is easily identified by Cops Hill, which rises above it. Rich in early history, as well as the recent history of the War of Independence, many historical buildings await visitors. As the most northern point on Shawmut Peninsula, it is just a stone's throw across the channel to Charles Town.

Off to the extreme south end, keen eyes will just barely make out a low lying narrow spit of land that has a single road flanked on the west by the Charles River and on the right by the sea. This narrow strip of land, appropriately called the "Neck," connects the city to the mainland. For seafarers who arrive at high tide, the Neck will be hidden by waves that lap at its roadway, but if your arrival is at low tide, stinking mudflats extend for hundreds of yards to either side. At its far end, where the Neck joins the mainland, early Bostonians built a conspicuous, heavily fortified gate to guard the entrance to the city.

sails directly into the harbor. First-time visitors instinctively gesture at the tall white spires of the city's most prominent historical monuments, while those familiar with the city call out their names: North Church, Old South Meeting House, and State House. It is at this point that it becomes clear to everyone on board that Boston is more than a city; it is a city that occupies the entire Shawmut Peninsula connected to the mainland at the south end by only a narrow spit of land known as "Boston Neck," but more commonly simply called the "Neck."

Arriving by Horse and Wagon

For fellow Americans interested in joining Bostonians this Fourth of July and getting here faster, safer, and cheaper than by boat, a network of roads suitable for horse and wagon leads to the city. Travelers from the larger cities to the south will find travel especially convenient because they will be able to use the Boston Post Road. As the name suggests, this road was initially designed for post

riders, that is, those who carry the mail. In 1772 the road was enlarged and improved to accommodate wagon and commercial stagecoach service. Today's travelers can choose between three different routes, all of which connect Boston with New York, but each of which passes through different cities between the two cosmopolitan cities. Patriots who marched with General Washington during the war will remember these roads well. From New York to Boston by commercial coach in good weather is a seven-day adventure.

The advantages to choosing the Post Road over the smaller footpaths are

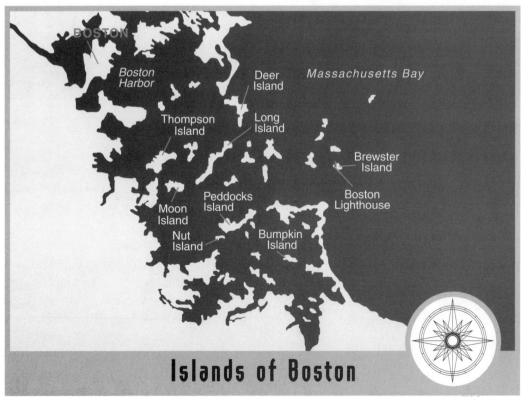

Islands of Boston

Traveling to Boston by stagecoach is easy and convenient. Visitors who take the Post Road from New York will enjoy a comfortable seven-day-long ride.

many. Most evident is the width and smoothness of this road — it is sufficient to accommodate carriage and wagon traffic with considerable comfort compared to older and less maintained roads. One English visitor named Margaret Hall, who took one of the smaller roads but will surely take the Post Road next time, had this to say about her journey:

We jolted up here yesterday at the rate of four hours to thirteen miles and quite fast enough for the safe of one's bones, for such a road for ruts and hoes and all manner of conveniences for shaking poor mortals to pieces I have not traveled over since I crossed the Pyrenees. . . . And away we went bumping, thumping, jolting, shaking, tossing and tumbling over the wickedest road, I do think, that ever wheel rumbled upon.[9]

The Post Road is also the safer of the two options. It has a sufficient flow of traffic, which deters highwaymen from robbing travelers. Equally important is the engineering of the road, which accommodates wet winter travel thanks to flat wood beams that lay side-by-side along the length of the trail and are embedded in the road surface. Coaches traveling these so-called corduroy or washboard roads enjoy better traction and are less apt to become mired in mud.

Travelers on a tight budget, without a horse or the money to purchase a stagecoach ticket, can rent horses. One way to save money, yet speed a journey along faster than on foot, is for two people to rent a horse and use the "ride and tie" method of travel. This ingenious system of sharing a horse works like this: One person starts out on the horse while the other walks. After an agreed-upon distance, the rider dismounts and ties the horse to a secure object such as a tree or post at a known tavern. When the one who started out walking locates the horse, he mounts it and rides past the first rider, who is now walking, to the next tying point. In this fashion, each person rides half the way and walks the other half.

A Safe and Modern City

However it is guests find their way here, each will be amazed at the work that has been done to secure and modernize the city. Everyone can feel perfectly safe wandering streets, night and day. In keep-

ing with the English model of ensuring the public's safety, two groups of law enforcement officers patrol the streets around the clock. During the night, security is provided by a group of men called the "night watch." You will be able to pick them out in a crowd by the badges they wear and the five-foot-long black staff each carries complete with a

Visitors can feel safe knowing that night watchmen like this one patrol Boston's dark streets.

five-inch solid brass ball at one end for cracking the skulls of wrongdoers.

During daylight hours, another group called the "constables" provides the same duties in addition to serving warrants and arresting lawbreakers. A particular concern of theirs is the reckless discharge of firearms, as this Boston law indicates: "If any person fires off a piece [pistol] after the watch is set, he shall be fined or be whipped."[10] One of the reasons the constables are so efficient at their jobs is because if they are not prompt and efficient at executing their duties, they themselves are fined.

Streetlights are the most recent of the city's modern approaches to making streets safe and enjoyable at night. A few of the main streets downtown along the wharf, such as Marlborough, Orange, Newberry, King, Milk, and Ann, are popular avenues for tourists and have been fitted with streetlights that burn whale oil. One of the jobs of the night watch is to light the wicks in the evening and extinguish them before they go off duty at sunrise.

Fires are another security problem that have plagued the city. Today, in response to the need to reduce their destructive impact, a variety of fire laws have been written and an organized fire department has been created. Following Boston's great fire of 1711, the city councilmen,

 ## Boston Fires

Fire has played a major role in the history of Boston. Since the founding of the city in 1630, several major fires have swept the city, each time changing the skyline and redefining the design of the wards and streets. Many of the historic buildings that played pivotal roles in the War of Independence had been destroyed and rebuilt at least once before the war. The State House that we know today is actually the third one to stand on its present site; the first having been destroyed by the great fire of 1711 and the second destroyed by fire in 1748.

Although all Bostonians suffered losses from fires, the city gradually learned to improve its fire control tactics and equipment. After the fire in 1676, for example, Boston purchased a new pump engine and hired Thomas Atkins and twelve other men to fight fires. These men are the first paid firefighters in the United States. The fire of 1711, which destroyed one-third of the city, including 110 family homes, was actually the city's eighth significant fire. Following this fire, wood salvaged from the hundreds of homes and shops was put to good use to build the Long Wharf.

Another innovation to grow out of this fire was the creation of the Mutual Fire Societies, each of which consists of about twenty neighbors banded together to help each other fight fires and salvage the contents of their homes. Each member of the society responds to the alarm with buckets, a bed key (to dismantle the owner's bed, the most valued piece of furniture), and a salvage bag bearing the society's emblem for collecting valuables.

whom we call the "selectmen," passed several laws in an effort to control fires. One law requires all houses and buildings to be built of stone or brick, and another requires a space between buildings that functions as a fire break. This critical space must be wide enough to accommodate at least two, and in some cases four, horses side-by-side. Because of the fire break law, today's major avenues measure between sixteen and twenty-four feet wide.

The selectmen also divided the city into fire districts and established the Fire Society. Each member of the Fire Society must own three water buckets for use in bucket brigades. In addition to the bucket brigades, the city has horse-drawn water wagons with pumps, each of which is operated by a crew of four men with broad backs capable of hand-pumping a stream of water through leather hoses to the top of three-story buildings.

The importance of clean water was another modernizing issue addressed by the city's selectmen following the war.

Until last year, all potable water in Boston came from one of the city's many local wells, rain barrels placed under the eves of private homes, and the spring on the Boston Common that is available to anyone willing to carry heavy jugs back home. Now, however, a few districts receive a continuous supply of clean water delivered from the Jamaica Pond, four miles south of the city, through a system of wood pipes made from tree trunks set below the streets. Although it will be years until city officials can guarantee the entire city clean water, travelers staying in the finer inns can now trust the water.

With few reasons to be concerned for one's safety, it is time for every visitor to focus on getting to know Boston. The city has a wealth of cultural activities worth exploring, interesting places to sleep and eat during your visit, and a whole host of fascinating idiosyncrasies that set the city apart from all others. In short, Boston is a city organized and eager to accommodate every traveler's needs and interests.

Chapter 3

First Day: Getting Around, Where to Stay, What to Eat

Everything in Boston is within sight, smell, and sound of the sea. All of the city's sixteen thousand residents live and work within a half mile of water. Relatively small for a major city, the Shawmut Peninsula is only 783 acres; just slightly larger than one square mile. First-time guests will enjoy exploring the streets of the city because, except for those at the base of the Tramount region, they are flat. Nonetheless, some will tire from an active day of meandering the curving, narrow cobblestone lanes and long, wide boulevards that crisscross the city. Unlike other cities, Boston provides newcomers with many landmarks that act as sentinels. Just tilt your head upward to locate one of the many tall church spires or one of the hilltops in the Tramount area—especially Beacon Hill. As soon as you spot and recognize one of these landmarks, the rest of the city snaps into perspective.

Another recommendation to help first-time guests locate historical sites is to purchase a map of the city. Several are available; some were drawn by Bostonians, some by English engineers before the war. Knowing the location of a few of the more interesting districts for tourism will speed one's journey and help locate the most direct route when asking for directions. Pick up a map of Boston at one of the city's bookstores; a good one to try is the Corner Book Store, appropriately located at the corner of School and Cornhill Streets. As the maps indicate, Boston is divided into twelve districts called "wards," a convenience that helps first-time visitors find places and follow directions. As soon as you have a sense of the layout of the city and its wards, it is time for an initial foray down Boston's many streets of excitement.

Getting Around the City

Boston is one of the world's great cities for walking. Although residential streets are narrow, most of the primary streets along the wharf areas in wards five, six, seven, and eight are paved with cobblestones and broad enough for easy travel. Many have raised sidewalks that separate pedestrians from horses.

The thrill of exploration is heightened by the view of the ocean on all sides, a characteristic that lends a unique and beautiful aspect to the city. As walkers take in the sights, smells, and sounds, they may also marvel at the

Wide, paved streets make walking a great way to explore the city.

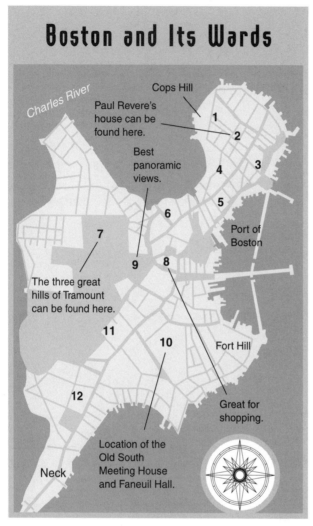

Boston and Its Wards

Charles River

Cops Hill

Paul Revere's house can be found here.

1

2

Best panoramic views.

4

3

5

6

Port of Boston

7

9   8

The three great hills of Tramount can be found here.

11

10

Fort Hill

12

Great for shopping.

Location of the Old South Meeting House and Faneuil Hall.

Neck

sula, the city would be an island were it not for the Neck that connects it to the mainland. To the west of the Neck lie large mudflats and marshes; beyond, the Charles River flows into Boston Harbor and separates the peninsula from Charles Town to the north. The east side of Boston is defined by a deep cove that divides the city's North and South Ends. Between Fort Hill in the South End and Cops Hill in the North End, a ridge of hills rises out of the ground, as described in 1634 by William Wood: "A high mountain with three little rising hills on top of it, wherefore it is called the Tramount."[11]

Ferry boats are available for trips around the perimeter of the city and across the north harbor to Charles Town and west up the Charles River to Cambridge. At the extreme north end, adjacent to a small cobblestone city square that is lined with shops, lies the harbor's edge, which is also marked by a granite quayside and several small stone wharves. From here, at the corner of Lynn and Charles Streets, the Winnisimmet ferries depart. Ticket prices are set by the city so there is no need to worry about being cheated. A trip halfway down the harbor to Long Wharf costs four copper pennies, all the way to the South End costs double. The

beauty of the distant bucolic country vistas to the south, west, and north, and beautiful sunrises to the east over the Atlantic. Before venturing out, here are a few helpful bits of information that will make everyone's visit the safest and most enjoyable possible.

One of the most interesting and unusual characteristics of Boston is its shape. Located entirely on the Shawmut Penin-

cost to cross over the half-mile strait to Charles Town is also regulated by the city, as this law indicates:

He [Edward Convers, the ferry owner] is allowed to take his wonted fees, namely, 2d. [pennies] for a single person and 1d. [penny] apiece if there be more than one; and for every horse and cow with the man that goeth with them, 6d., and for a goat 1d., and for a swine 2d., and if any shall desire to pass before light in the morning, or if it is after dark in the evening, he may take recompense answerable o the season and his pains and hazards, so it be not excessive.[12]

 # Private Turnpikes

Vacationers preferring to travel to and from Boston by road now have an alternative to the Boston Post Road and the dozens of small backwoods trails. A consortium of business leaders pooled their finances and built a turnpike to the city. This turnpike has the advantage of being a modern, high-quality road with the one disadvantage that it charges a toll to all who use it.

Boston Turnpike Fare Schedule
from Massachusetts General Act

Coach, chariot, phaeton, or outher four-wheel spring carriage	.25
drawn by two horses (additional horses 2¢ a piece)	.25
Wagons drawn by two horses (additional horses 2¢ a piece)	.10
Cart or wagon drawn by two oxen	.10
Curricle [light two-horse two-wheeled carriage]	.15
Chaise, chair, sulky, or other carriage for pleasure drawn by one horse	12.5
Cart, wagon, or truck drawn by one horse	.0625
Man and horse	.04
Sleigh or sled drawn by one horse	.04
Horses, mules, or neat cattle, led or driven, each	.01
Sheep or swine by the dozen	.03

Carts or wagons having wheels, the fellies (wheel rim) of which shall be Six Inches broad or more, shall be subject to pay only half the toll which carts or wagons otherwise constructed, shall be liable to pay.

Patrons examine a shopkeeper's merchandise. Because of Boston's lack of a formal banking system, exchanging currency can be a bit complicated.

For those more trusting of ground transport, hackney coaches (four-wheeled two-horse carriages) are available for hire. Most congregate in the busy wharf area and a good hearty shout of "hack!" will get a driver's attention.

Paying for Goods and Services

For sightseers arriving from England or from many of the rural inland towns along the New England seaboard, making purchases and paying for meals and rooms is a bit complicated because of America's recent independence. English guests arriving with their currency of pounds, shillings, and pence must exchange their one-pound silver coins and paper notes for 3.3 American silver dollars or 3.3 Spanish silver dollars, which are far more common. The city has not yet set up a formal banking system, which makes for some inconvenience, but when a few simple rules are followed, money exchanges work out just fine.

During your stay in Boston, remember two rules about money. First, try to refrain from offering English money to anyone. Although the war has been over for ten years, feelings of resentment toward the Royal Family still run deep and the sight of English money is an insult to most loyal Bostonians. Second, never accept "continentals," paper money printed by the Continental Congress during the revolution, as change from merchants. When the Revolutionary War broke out, the Continental Congress issued paper money to finance the war. Since the Congress had no power of taxation, these notes were backed by anticipated future tax revenues.

The front view of a six dollar bill.

Our young and inexperienced country issued far too much continental currency, causing it to depreciate rapidly. By the end of the war, it had become worthless—or, as the saying goes, "not worth a continental." If an unscrupulous merchant offers them as change, insist on change either in silver or trade more merchandise instead of taking the change.

At the present time, Boston establishments are happy to accept three different types of silver coins: Spanish silver dollars called "pieces of eight," the Spanish silver dollar called the "Pillar," and the recently minted American silver dollar. Perhaps the most interesting of the three coins is the pieces of eight, so named because Bostonians regularly cut the coin into eight pie-shape wedges called "bits" in order to make change. Two bits equal a quarter of a dollar; four bits, a half dollar; and six bits, three quarters of a dollar. To put the value of a dollar into

The back view of a six dollar bill.

perspective, the wage of most unskilled workers on the docks and in taverns is about one hundred silver dollars a year.

The other Spanish dollar, the Pillar, is perfectly rounded and far better minted than the older pieces of eight. The Pillar has been a legal tender dollar in Boston for many years and it took its name from an engraving on one of its sides, which depicts the Pillars of Gibraltar, where Spanish ships embarked from Mediterranean waters bound for England, America, and South America. The other side of the coin depicts the lions of the city of León, Spain, and the castles of Castile, Spain.

More rare, and more favored, in the city is the American silver dollar. This coin, first minted in 1776, is known for its consistent silver content, which is 99 percent pure silver and a consistent weight of one ounce. This coin is minted in Philadelphia and intentionally patterned after the Spanish pieces of eight coins. However, with the minting of other, smaller coins such as the half dollar, quarter dollar, and the copper penny, Bostonians have no need to cut the American silver dollar into bits.

For our wealthier visitors, proper gentlemen may want to carry gold coins in their pockets. These coins reduce the weight of coin purses and

NEW-ENGLAND: Nº 98.

THE BoftonGazette

Publifhed by Authority.

From MONDAY October 2. to MONDAY October 9. 1721.

By His Excellency
SAMUEL SHUTE Efq;
Captain General and GOVERNOUR in Chief,
in and over His Majefty's Province of the
Maffachufetts Bay in New-England, &c.
A Proclamation for a General
THANKSGIVING.

Orajmuch as amidft the various awful
Rebukes of Heaven, with which we are
righteoufly afflicted, in the Contagious
and Mortal Sicknefs among us, efpeci-
ally in the Town of Bofton ; The long and im-
moderate Rains, which have been fo hurtful to the
Husbandry and Fifhery ; And the threatning
Afpect of Affairs with Refpect to our Frontiers :
We are ftill under the higheft and moft indifpen-
fible Obligations of Gratitude for the many In-
ftances of the Divine Goodnefs in the Favours
vouchfafed to us in the Courfe of the Year paft ;
Particularly, For the LIFE of our Gracious Sovereign Lord the KING, Their Royal Highneffes
the Prince and Princefs of Wales and their Iffue,
and the increafe of the Royal Family ; The Pre-
fervation of His Majefty's Kingdoms and Do-
minions from the terrible and defolating Pefti-
lence, which hath for fo long a time been wafting
the Kingdom of France ; And the happy Succefs
of His Majefty's Wife Counfils for Reftoring and
Confirming the Peace of Europe ; For the Conti-
nuance of our valuable Privileges, both Civil and
Ecclefiaftical ; and the Divine Bleffing upon this
Government in their Adminiftrations ; Particularly, In fucceeding the Methods taken to prevent
the Infults of the Eaftern Indians ; For giving
fo great a Meafure of Health within this Province, and Moderating the Mortality of the
Small Pox, fo that a great Number of Perfons
are Recovered from that Diftemper ; And for
granting us fo comfortable a former Harveft,
and fo hopeful a Profpect of the latter :

I Have therefore thought fit with the Advice
of His Majefty's Council, to Order and Appoint
Thurfday the Twenty fixth Inftant, to be
Obferved as a Day of Publick THANKS-
GIVING throughout this Province, ftrictly
forbidding all Servile Labour thereon, and ex-
horting both Minifters and People in their re-

pective Affemblies on the faid Day, to offer up
humble and fincere THANKS to Almighty GOD,
for His many Favours, as aforefaid, and for
many other Bleffings beftowed on a finful People.

Given at Bofton, the Eighteenth Day of Sep-
tember, 1721. And in the Eighth Year of
the Reign of Our Sovereign Lord GEORGE,
by the Grace of GOD of Great Britain,
France and Ireland, KING, Defender of the
Faith, &c.

By Order of the Governour,
with Advice of the Council.
J. Willard, Sect.   S. SHUTE.

GOD Save the KING.

The following Advices from Foreign Parts
are taken from the Weekly Journal of
July 22.

Letters from France ftill are very full of the
Preparations making for the Congrefs of Cambray, and
of bringing the long Contention between Spain and the
Allies, to a fpeedy Conclufion. However, notwithftand-
ing the great Hurry they feem juft now to be in upon this
expected Treaty is to begin, nor let us into the Reafon
for its being delayed ; fo that we are much in the dark
about this Affair ; and confidering the uncertain Situation
of Things, if we fhould continue fo for fome time
longer yet, it would be no manner of Surprize to us.
We can really fee nothing in our Accounts, that can
afford us any Satisfaction as to the Plague in France ; for
tho' much has been pretended this Week to the contrary, it does not appear to us to have abated any thing of
its former Fury, as with much Affurance has been given
out. If the Violence of it has been lefs in one Part,
it has, as was faid in our laft, been for want of frefh Ob-
jects to prey upon ; and the Fury with which it has
broke out anew, in the Courfe of its dreadful Progrefs,
has made it fufficiently evident, that upon the whole,
the Devaftations continue equally great to what the
Diftemper ever occafioned fince it came to its Height.
And indeed if we confider the fure Footing it has got,
the vaft Number of People and Places infected, and allow
the Contagion to be of to malignant a Nature as it has
all along been reprefented to us, 'twill be much more un-
expected, as 'tis really more improbable, to find it abating,
and growing lefs, during the violent hot Weather which
is now in France, than to hear that it proceeds in the
fame outrageous Manner it has already done, till after
the Summer Seafon is over, and the Cold fets in to check
its Advances.

---

sure it passes the test of soft pure gold. These coins are quite rare and none are minted in America. Users should be prepared ahead of time to negotiate their change in silver simply because converting the value of gold to silver is a tricky proposition.

Once money has been exchanged, it is time to find a good place to sleep and to grab a bite to eat. Here in Boston, you will find three types of what the locals collectively call "public houses." It is important to know the differences between them because each operates differently. An inn implies a place to spend the night and possibly get a light breakfast the morning after; a tavern is a place of food and evening entertainment; and an ordinary is a tavern where a simple ordinary meal is offered at a set time and price to the public.

prevent dirty fingers or gloves because merchants wash gold coins before distribution to customers. If you receive one of these coins, expect to see many prominent "chop marks" around the edge. These marks are actually indentations from the teeth of merchants and customers who bite into the coin to be

Boston's Inns

The best sources of information for inns in Boston are the post riders who deliver mail throughout the new country. All mail is delivered to a post house, which is always a public gathering place such as a tavern or inn. Since their rides take them long distances, post riders know most of the inns. In addition to delivering mail to the inns, they also sleep at them. Reservations are recommended for some of the more popular inns. The cost to contact them depends on where visitors live. Present postal costs render the following: under 30 miles, 6 cents; between 30 and 60 miles, 8 cents; and between 60 and 150 miles, 12 cents.

Inns are plentiful in Boston and suit nearly every visitor's budget. Be forewarned, however, that even the very best inns may not be suitable for wealthy travelers accustomed to separate and elegant accommodations. Upper-crust travelers should find rooms with friends and relatives. Boston is still recovering from years of war, and it will be many more years before it can

Boston has an inn to fit every budget. Travelers must only decide how much they want to spend.

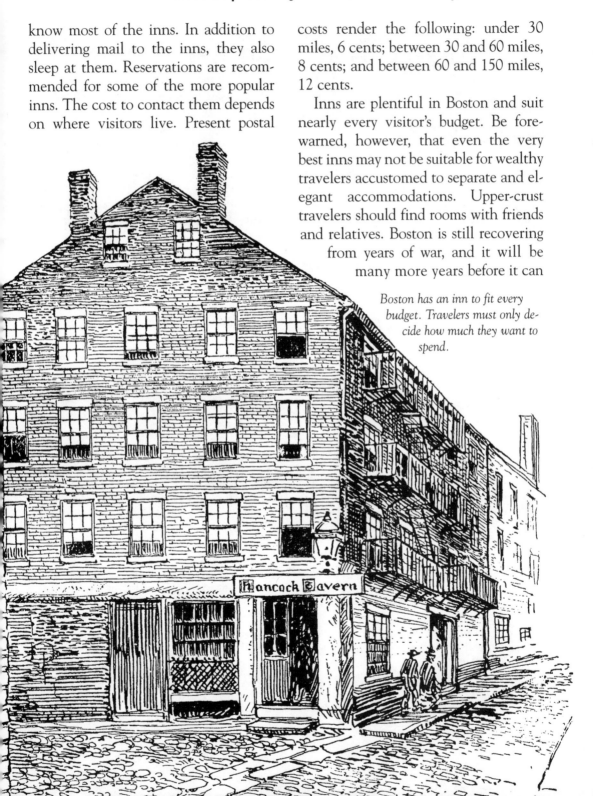

Elegant Dining

Occasionally, well-heeled gourmands want to sit down to an elegant meal far beyond the means of ordinary taverns. Fortunately for guests seeking such a graceful experience, a handful of taverns cater to fine diners. Expect to spend between one and one-and-a-half dollars for a complete dinner for two. The cost is high, and the food excellent, but the real difference between elegant taverns and all the others is the sophisticated ambience.

The first thing diners experience at upper-class taverns is the decorum. The dining room is filled with lively yet quiet conversation, and the wait staff equals the number of diners; three times the number found at most taverns. The room is filled with fresh flowers when they are in season; all tables are covered with ironed linen tablecloths; lace and colorful curtains cover all windows to reduce any drafts; and during the winter, a blazing fire warms the room.

After being seated by the hostess, drinks are presented to each guest, ladies first, on a serving tray. Next, waiters take each guest's order. Ladies never order anything for themselves and, therefore, never engage in any conversation with the waiters. The gentleman next to the lady takes responsibility for ordering her meal and also asks the server for more wine as her glass empties. Waiters at finer taverns are neither to be seen nor heard. Much of their time is spent standing like statues in wait of an unobtrusive signal from the hostess to proceed with the next task.

Multicourse dinners are an important social event and last for several hours. Following the first two courses of soup and salad, the tablecloth is replaced by a fresh one before the main course arrives. To present the main course, servers place one entrée before each guest and diners pass their plates and serve one another from the dish nearest them. When each plate has been filled, the guests stop passing them and eat from whichever is before them. Conversation is usually lively, yet not loud enough to interrupt other diners. Waiters silently refill wine and water glasses, offer fresh linen napkins, and replace spoons and knives without being asked. Following the clearing of the main course dishes, the tablecloth is removed, and dessert plates are presented on the bare wood table. Following toasts at the end of the meal, the ladies typically adjourn to the parlor for tea while gentlemen remain at the table for several more rounds of drinks before rejoining the ladies.

satisfy every customer. Today, Boston innkeepers offer three levels of inns: stylish, moderate, and modest.

Stylish inns, found around the base of the Tramount district, cost guests as much as one dollar a night per room. Innkeepers pride themselves in claiming that visitors will be as comfortable at their inn as they are in their own homes. Guests can expect to enjoy their own rooms, soft goose-down beds, either candles or a whale-oil lamp, a washbasin with fresh water and clean linens, and an indoor privy shared with the other guests. A breakfast of fresh buttermilk rolls with honey, a slab of salted or sugared ham, sweet potatoes fried in goose lard, and ample tea is included in the cost of a night's stay. A limited number of inns also stable horses for the night.

Moderate inns, costing between a quarter dollar and a half dollar, provide a safe, warm place to sleep with a simple breakfast in the morning but not much in the way of finery. If a family with children stays in one, they will be able to have a room of their own. Men traveling alone, however, might go to sleep alone but wake up in the morning to find roommates sleeping in nearby beds. Such was the experience of Dr. Hamilton, who woke up one morning to discover:

Two beds in the room, besides that in which I lay, in one of which lay two great hulking fellows, with long black beards, having their own hair, and not so much as half a night cap twixt both of them. In the other bed was a raw-boned boy, who, with the two lubbers [distasteful persons], huddled on his clothes, who in the morning went reeling down-stairs, making as much noise as three horses.[13]

The owners of Boston's modest inns, for those on a tight budget, expect travelers to share a bed with one or more fellow travelers. This is a practical solution during cold weather because few blankets are available and more people in a bed make for a warmer night's sleep. The accommodations are crude and may include wood pallets, burlap sacks stuffed with straw, and a blanket. It is recommended that men who stay in such inns sleep with their money under their person.

Taverns

Favorite Boston taverns that serve the local and traveling public good food, strong liquors, and lively evening entertainment include the Bunch of Grapes, the Bell-in-Hand, the Green Dragon, the Indian Queen, and the Copper Bull. Most taverns are licensed to sell food; to serve alcoholic drinks such as beer, ale, wine, cider, brandy, and rum; and to provide gambling sports such as darts, cockfights, and games of chance involving cards and dice.

Look for their colorful and entertaining signs that hang over their doorways as you walk down the street. Each sign gives newcomers some idea of what they serve, how much food costs, and the tavern's desired patrons. These carved wood signs are works of art that use a combination of pictures, such as platters of food, and various symbols of status to indicate desired customers. One such sign might show a platter of breads and soups with a fishing boat surrounded by a coil of rope, indicating simple inexpensive food for working-class folks. Another sign might depict pheasant and duck roasting on a spit, a billiards table, and race horses along the bottom, indicating pricey meals intended for well-heeled Bostonians. These signs are especially important for the majority of the population who remain illiterate.

Inside, tavern owners attempt to create the most pleasant and attractive atmosphere possible. Each tavern has its own personality. Many have several rooms, such as the tap room, reserved just for drinking; a game room that offers a variety of entertainments; a parlor room with comfortable chairs for quiet conversation; a billiards room within elegant taverns; and always somewhere on the premises, a fireplace by which guests can warm up in the winter. A few taverns, most notably the ramshackle Green Dragon, have enriched the city's recent history as establishments where leaders of the revolution gathered to discuss strategies against the king.

Regardless of the interior design, food is at the heart of the tavern. All foods are locally grown. The principal difference between the expensive and inexpensive fare is the meat. Taverns

Patrons drink and dine at a Boston tavern. These establishments offer varied menus to appeal to rich and poor alike.

Men gather outside the Green Dragon Tavern, one of the city's most famous spots and the place where patriot leaders often met to discuss strategies for the Revolution.

catering to the rich feature the most tender cuts of beef, as well as mutton, pheasant, duck, an array of fish, shellfish chowder, several types of squash, potatoes, a variety of berry pie desserts, and almond pudding. Taverns that attract working-class customers keep on hand venison; sausages; a variety of calf organs such as liver, brain, and tongue; cod; oysters; chicken; pigeon; fried apples; macaroons; orange pudding; and pumpkin pie. Alcoholic drinks are sold to adults only; children enjoy a selection of coffee, tea, cider, and chocolate drinks.

Once the essentials are taken care of, it is time you discover what Boston has to offer that can not be found in any other city. We suggest guests become acquainted with the significant role the city played in the recent War of Independence. To do this, set aside at least one day to visit Boston's four most significant historical landmarks.

Chapter 4

Four Historic Landmarks

Boston has many historic land-marks that played pivotal roles in the War of Independence. The four most significant, all of which can be visited in a single day of casual walking, are North Church, Faneuil Hall, the State House, and Old South Meeting Hall. To make this walking tour as convenient as possible, start at the North Church in ward number two in the North End and work your way south.

North Church

Begun in 1723, North Church, which is correctly called Christ Church in the City of Boston, sits at the far north end of the city on Salem Street, just two blocks west of North Street. Completed in 1747, it is today the oldest church in the city, a distinction it inherited after an older church, which locals still refer to as Old North Church, was torn down by the English army for firewood during the winter of 1775–1776. The North Church you see today is easily recognized by its Georgian architecture, modeled after a church in London that was de-signed by that city's renowned architect Christopher Wren.

The great church will be spotted long before sightseers arrive on Salem Street. Its 191-foot-tall steeple is the highest in the city. Painted white, it is intended to function as a beckoning landmark to guide ships far out to sea into the safety of Boston Harbor. This same steeple played a major role at the outbreak of the War of Independence in 1775 when the church sexton, Robert Newman, climbed the steeple and hanged two lanterns the night before the first battle of the war in Concord, thereby warning of an English attack by sea.

The church itself is made of wood from the forests of Maine and red bricks baked in kilns in the nearby town of Medford. Seventy feet in length, fifty-one feet in breadth, and forty-two feet to the top of the belfry, it is a testament to the master craftsmen who constructed it.

Visitors are encouraged to climb up to the twenty-four-foot square brick belfry that supports the white wood steeple. Here you will find the eight bells that have played an important role in the city's spiritual and political life. An inscription tells the tourist, "We are the first bells cast for the British Empire in North America."[14] Although these bells are principally rung to summon parishioners each Sunday morning, they also played a significant role as signal bells during the war. Bostonians recognize the sounds of these bells, which have a distinctive sound compared to other city bells, and the ringing of the bells also signals noteworthy events such as deaths, a city fire, enemy invasions, and of course the end of war. On November 25, 1783, these bells rang up and down the scales, conveying great joy and announcing the end of the war.

Upon entering the church, guests get a feel for its large size. It can accommodate 350 parishioners in its pew boxes. The pew boxes, with their three-foot-high wood sides, are designed to keep worshipers warm in the winter. Many parishioners bring with

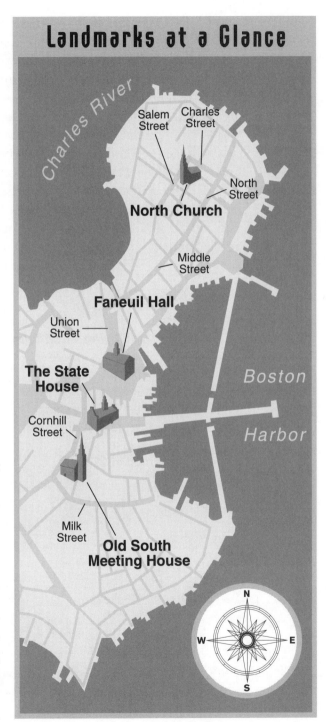

Landmarks at a Glance

Charles River

Salem Street

Charles Street

North Street

North Church

Middle Street

Faneuil Hall

Union Street

The State House

Cornhill Street

Boston

Harbor

Milk Street

Old South Meeting House

N
W   E
S

them foot warmers filled with hot coals or stones for additional heat. Each Sunday at the tolling of the bells, families throughout the north end file in and take their places in their family boxes. As you wander the boxes, you will see small attached brass plates bearing the names of well-to-do north end Boston families that sit at their nameplates each Sunday.

Many of these names are famous families that made their money as shipbuilders, ship captains, merchants, and importers and exporters.

The two brass chandeliers, gifts of Captain William Maxwell, hang above the central aisle of the church and each bears twelve candles that are lit for afternoon and evening services. As you exit the church, find your way back to North Street, make a right turn, and continue walking south until North Street turns into Middle Street. After four blocks, turn left on Union Street and continue two more blocks. There the street opens onto a public square called Market Square by some and Dock Square by others. Whatever you choose to call it, in the center stands the second imposing historic monument on the tour, Faneuil Hall.

North Church

Bell Tower and Steeple
The place where Robert Newman hung his lanterns, the tower contains the first set of church bells in North America, cast in 1745.

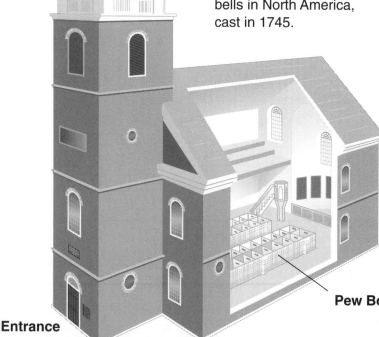

Pew Boxes

Entrance

Faneuil Hall

Sightseers will find the red brick Faneuil Hall one of the most colorful and energetic locations in the city. You cannot miss this long, two-story red brick building with its banks of tall windows that bathe the interior in sunlight. If you are still in doubt, step back and look up for its distinctive

The Layout of the City

Boston is well organized, and by purchasing and studying the city map drawn by Osgood Carleton (sold for just a penny) the order of the city will become obvious.

One of the advantages of Carleton's map is that it identifies the twelve wards, into which the city is cleverly organized. Each ward has both a name and a number, but locals use only the numbers when referring to them. The best shopping ward, for example, is number eight, located by the central wharf. The best panoramic view of the city, on the other hand, is in ward nine, the district around Beacon Hill. Knowing the wards will come in handy if you need to ask directions. Local Bostonians use them all the time, so it is a good idea to know some of them. It is easy to learn ward locations because ward numbers are assigned in a logical geographical order beginning with ward number one on the north end and ending with ward number twelve at the south end.

The map also introduces first-time visitors to our streets and their names. As your map indicates, Bostonians travel both straight and curved streets. The streets curve around the hills' bases, but are long and straight along the flat areas close to the water. Some streets run most of the length of the city, but do not keep the same name. Long streets change names every five or six blocks to assist people in finding homes and businesses because houses and buildings are not numbered. The city's longest street that runs from the center of town in ward eight to the south end in ward twelve, as an example, begins as Cornhill Street, then becomes Marlborough, then Newbury, and finally Orange. Although this may be a bit confusing, those with a quick wit will recognize that this naming convention is always alphabetical by direction.

Boston's State House is easy to find in ward ten.

Boston's legendary Faneuil Hall dominates Market Square. The hall's historic significance and lively marketplace make it a must-see for travelers.

grasshopper weather vane perched on top of the building's cupola.

This elegant building was built in 1742 by Peter Faneuil, a successful merchant, who dedicated it to the citizens of Boston because he saw the need for a building that could function as a public assembly hall and downtown marketplace. Faneuil stipulated that the ground floor be used for the selling of food and housewares and the second floor used as a town hall for public discussion and debate. Tragically the hall was severely damaged by fire in 1761. The Faneuil Hall before you, which remains true to

the original design, replaced the original hall in 1762.

Getting into the marketplace is half the fun of coming here. The streets surrounding the hall are jammed with carts that carry all manner of produce, grains, meats, fowl, and fish. All meats are isolated at the west end of the building so the butchers can wash down the stalls each evening to maintain proper sanitation. With close access to the wharf, goods are carted directly from the boats to be sold. There is barely room to squeeze between the carts and horses because merchants who are not able to rent space inside have set up temporary stalls outside, flying colorful pennants on the sidewalks surrounding the hall to get shoppers' interests. Do not be put off by the jostling atmosphere. Charge right in like one of the locals, but at the same time hold your money tightly—this is a favorite spot for pickpockets. Once you make your way inside to the ground floor, the bountiful array of goods available coupled with the shouts of merchants and the screaming gulls swooping down to snatch bits of scattered food create a thrilling atmosphere.

Take the stairs at either end of the hall to the second floor to experience where much of our new nation's early history was made. It is here, in this great room, that colonists first protested the Sugar Act and established the doctrine at the heart of America's revolution by refusing to pay taxes without legal representation. It was here, too, that firebrand Samuel Adams rallied the citizens of Boston to the cause of independence from Great Britain, and it was here that General George Washington toasted the nation on its first birthday. For all of these reasons, this second floor meeting hall has been dubbed America's "Cradle of Liberty."

Samuel Adams.

To get to the third stop on the tour, the State House, exit the south side of Faneuil Hall, walk one block south to King Street, turn right, and walk one more block. This puts you at the State House doorstep on the corner of King and Cornhill Streets.

The State House

This august, three-story wood-and-brick edifice was built in 1713 to house the government offices of the Massachusetts Bay Colony. It is one of the more distinctive buildings in Boston because of its great profile (113 feet by 37 feet) and for its cupola that towers 96 feet above the street. It stands on the site of Boston's Towne House, which burned in the great fire of 1711.

Prior to the Revolution, the council chamber of the royal governor was located on the third floor at the east end of the building, facing Long Wharf and the harbor. This room was his official place of governance and, as such, the room where he made most major decisions regulating the city while under English rule. As friction grew between Bostonians and the English, this room also became a place for heated debates and fiery rhetoric by dedicated patriots against the royal governor and the crown.

A Poem in Praise of Faneuil Hall

The importance of Faneuil Hall as a place for purchasing food and sparking the debate of revolution was summarized in an eighteenth-century poem written by F.W. Hatch and made available in Walter Whitehall's book, *Boston: A Topographical History:*

Bestir ye!
Peter Faneuil,
Old Frenchmen in your grave,
'Twas not for tourist folderol [nonsense]
Your deed of trust you gave.

You planned and gave
A Market Hall
Designed for honest trade,
With quarters up above, where men
Could call a spade a spade.

Here orators
In ages past
Have mounted their attack
Undaunted by proximity
Of sausage on the rack.

Men here have shouted,
Age on age,
With fervor for their cause,
And, going home, brought nourishment
To steel a freeman's jaws.

Let tourists come,
Let tourists go
And carry home belief
That Boston Patriots are backed
By Honest Yankee beef!

During one such speech in 1761, James Otis argued eloquently against the Writs of Assistance, the English policy which allowed the army to search homes without legal warrants. Otis lost the argument, but his impassioned speech was one of the events that led to the American Revolution. John Adams recalled in his journal, "Otis was a flame of fire . . . then and there the child Independence was born."[15]

Just prior to the war, the central area of the second floor was the meeting place of the Massachusetts Assembly, one of the most independent of the colonial legislatures. This assembly was the first legislative body in the colonies to call for sectional unity and the formation of an American Congress. Here you will see the visitor's gallery that was installed in 1766. This gallery was the first of its kind in the English-speaking world to permit common citizens to hear officials debate the important issues of the day.

Outside, at one end of the second floor, on the west side of the building overlooking King Street, visitors can see the small balcony, which has a flight of stairs that connects it to the street below. This balcony has a long history from which important proclamations have been read to the crowds below. The area directly below this historic balcony was the site of the Boston Massacre, which occurred on March 5, 1770. It was also from this balcony that the first public reading of the Declaration of Independence took place on July 18, 1776, by

Colonel Thomas Crafts and Sheriff William Greenleaf. Later that day, the lion and unicorn weather vane, along with other symbols of royal authority, were removed from the roof of the building and tossed into a great bonfire.

The State House also functions as a public meeting place for the exchange of economic and local news. A Merchant's Exchange still occupies the first floor and John Hancock and others still rent the basement for warehouse space. As the center of political life and thought in the colonies, the State House became one of the more important public buildings in Boston.

Still heading south, the last stop on the tour is the Old South Meeting Hall. Just two blocks away, go south on Cornhill one block where the street name changes to Marlborough and proceed one more block to Milk Street. Here, on the northeast corner, stands "Old South," as most Bostonians refer to it.

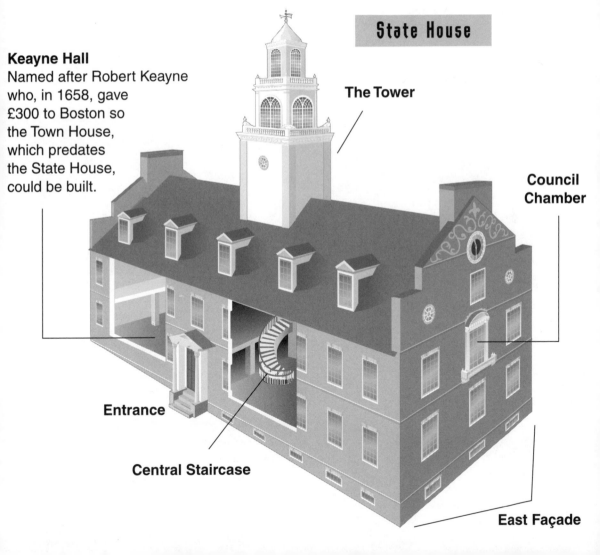

State House

Keayne Hall
Named after Robert Keayne who, in 1658, gave £300 to Boston so the Town House, which predates the State House, could be built.

The Tower

Council Chamber

Entrance

Central Staircase

East Façade

Paul Revere's House

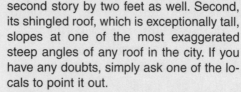

Located on North Square Street, a short one-block street off the larger North Street in ward number two, the home of Boston's great patriot Paul Revere is an interesting piece of architecture. It is located in one of Boston's oldest residential neighborhoods, the North End. Since the house has no house number, there are two ways to easily identify it: First, it is a two-story wood house whose upper story overhangs the lower story by about two feet on each side, and the roof, in turn, overhangs the second story by two feet as well. Second, its shingled roof, which is exceptionally tall, slopes at one of the most exaggerated steep angles of any roof in the city. If you have any doubts, simply ask one of the locals to point it out.

Revere's house was originally built in 1680 by Robert Howard, a wealthy merchant, on the site of the former parsonage of the Second Church of Boston that was destroyed in the great fire of 1676. Following Mr. Howard, the home was owned by several families before Revere purchased it in 1770. Although Howard was a wealthy man, this house is not extravagant; the basement and first floor are a combined 850 square feet and the second story is an additional 930 square feet.

You can catch glimpses of the home's interior through the windows from the street, but bear in mind that this house remains the private residence of Revere and his family. Please do not disturb their privacy. Through the windows you may be able to see the heavy beamed ceiling and two large fireplaces. Two large bedrooms are out of view, on the second floor. Tall curiosity seekers may be able to peer over the brick wall into the courtyard, where a beautiful garden is intersected by brick walkways.

Although still occupied by its owner, Paul Revere's house has become a popular stop for visitors.

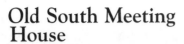

Old South Meeting House

Built of brick in 1729, Old South is a Puritan religious meeting house. Capable of accommodating six hundred worshipers in its large ground-floor meeting room and another two hundred on its three balconies, this is the largest room in Boston and the largest building as well.

As you enter, keep in mind that this is a religious meeting house even though it is never called a church.

The entire room is filled with pew boxes rented by Puritan families. Although brass nameplates are not used here as they are in North Church, each family knows its box and when the collection plate is passed, the money contributed is actually the rent for the box. Each box rents for a different amount, but most annual rents run between eighty-five and one hundred dollars, roughly the annual income for a common worker. Prime boxes, those most visible to the rest of the congregation, lie along the front close to the pulpit and along the outside aisles near the doors through which all enter and depart. Puritans with small incomes stand in the back balcony where they know the collection plate will not be passed.

Visiting historians are particularly interested in the Old South Meeting House because it holds great historical importance to all who experienced the difficult years leading up to the Revolution. On December 16, 1773, an angry group of Bostonians gathered at Faneuil Hall to protest the tea tax, and as their numbers

Boston's Old South Meeting House, located on Milk Street, has been a gathering place for both worshipers and revolutionaries.

55

grew, shouts of "Old South" rang out. The crowd wanted to reassemble here, just three blocks away, because the Old South Meeting House could better accommodate the overflowing emotional throng. As the meeting reconvened, five thousand angry colonists jammed inside and led by Samuel Adams, roundly denounced the tax. As the crescendo of voices rose, Adams stood and uttered the phrase, "This meeting can do nothing more to save the country."[16] Unbeknownst to most, this phrase was actually a code known only by a few Sons of Liberty, ordering them to prepare to board three tea ships tied up at Griffin's Wharf and to throw the tea into the harbor. Because of Adams's triggering words, this meeting house is considered the place where the "tea party" began. As revenge for this event, the English general Burgoyne tore out all pew boxes, burned them, and converted Old South into a riding academy for his troops.

General John Burgoyne.

In the event that your visit occurs around March 5, it is recommended that you take the time to visit the Old South to experience the annual commemoration of the Boston Massacre that took place that day in 1770. The building gets crowded with people who remember the terrible and bloody event that occurred just a short walk away from here. Each year, one of Boston's leading orators such as John Hancock or Dr. Joseph Warren delivers a stirring patriotic speech.

Chapter 5

Three Casual Walks

Boston is a walker's paradise. For those for whom visiting historic landmarks is not high on the list of favorite activities, a tour of three casual walks is recommended: Tramount, Boston Common, and the wharf. These walks comfortably fill one day.

First, take in a view of the city from the highest point, Tramount. Rising with surprising steepness across the middle of the city, west to east, stands this range of three hills, the tallest of which, Beacon Hill, stands between the two smaller ones. This alignment has for years prompted sailors to describe this ridge of hills as the outline of a man's head and shoulders. This is a great spot with a view that gives you a sense of just where you have been or where you may want to go before you begin walking the city.

To find your way to the base of the mountain, which is in ward number nine and just a couple of blocks north of Boston Common, walk to the east end of Beacon Street. As the tallest peak in the city, you cannot miss it.

Hike up Tramount

A hike to the crest of Tramount provides a breezy and spectacular panoramic view of the city. Simply follow the dirt footpath that winds its way up the hill. From the vantage point of the summit, standing next to the beacon on the 150-foot Beacon Hill, you can see the entire city laid out below.

At such a vantage point, you can spy all of the city's activities at a single glance. The harbor, not more than a half mile to the east, is filled with vessels of every size and design riding at anchor and waiting to load and unload cargo. Toward the south end, the neat grid of the streets is filled with commercial handcarts and horse-drawn wagons entering and leaving the city at the Neck. And in contrast to the rest of the city,

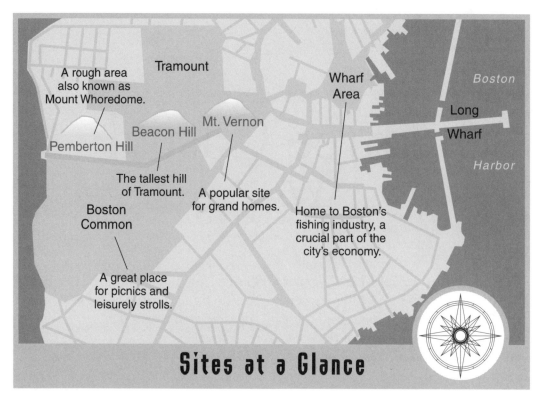

A rough area also known as Mount Whoredome.

Tramount

Wharf Area

Boston

Long Wharf

Mt. Vernon

Beacon Hill

Pemberton Hill

Harbor

The tallest hill of Tramount.

A popular site for grand homes.

Boston Common

Home to Boston's fishing industry, a crucial part of the city's economy.

A great place for picnics and leisurely strolls.

Sites at a Glance

just below and slightly off to the west is the quiet greenery of Boston Common.

Looking miles out to the east horizon, far from the city below, you can see ships entering and departing the harbor, maneuvering through the dozens of offshore islands. To the west, church steeples of many small towns dot the countryside amid fields of corn, barley, and rye, and the Charles and Mystic Rivers silently mingle with the waters of the Atlantic. One old-time resident described the Tramount vantage point as:

A high Mountaine with three little rising Hills on the top of it, wherefore it is called the Tramount. From the top of this Mountaine a man may over-looke all the islands which lie before the Bay, and discry such ships as are upon the Seacoast.[17]

Just below the beacon is a grand, old weathered house. Its once well-tended garden has fallen into neglect and its wooden fence leans almost on its side. The guards that watch over the beacon say the house is the oldest in Boston, built by a hermit who lived there before the Puritans arrived. Forced out, the hermit was said to have put a curse on the house, which has been vacant ever since.

The western shoulder of the Tramount, Pemberton Hill, is bare on its southern and western slopes, being quite steep, but the gentler northern slope is occupied by a seedy looking shantytown of shingled shacks, crumbling homes, and houses of low repute. The winding streets are often clogged with drunken soldiers, sailors, and old crusty sea dogs who swap sea stories. The pleasures offered here of gambling, alcohol, and prostitution have collectively earned this hill the infamous name of Mount Whoredome. It is best for proper folk to stay clear of this area because it is also a haunt for roughnecks in search of unsuspecting visitors.

The hill to the east of Beacon, Mount Vernon, is principally known for its barren slope, which provides an excellent view of the wharf. At its base, one can see a few stately homes of the wealthy that are beginning to define the style of the Tramount district. One of Boston's best young architects, Charles Bulfinch, who recently returned from two years of distinguished study in Europe, recommends that this hill be cut down and leveled to make way for even more elegant homes with spectacular views of the harbor. As part of this farsighted plan, Bulfinch proposes that the dirt removed from Mount Vernon can be used as fill in the bay, thereby increasing the size of the wharf to accommodate more ships.

A quick scramble down the hill puts hikers at the doorstep of the second stop on our casual walks, Boston Common, the city's most beautiful and most quiet spot.

The Boston Common

In the shadow of Tramount and edged by the Charles River to the west, you will come across a broad expanse of green

The Beacon on Beacon Hill

Bostonians erected the original Beacon Hill beacon to alert the city of a possible invasion by the French navy. Beacon Hill, which was originally called "Sentry Hill," became the selected site because, at 150 feet tall, it is the highest of the three Tramount hills. The beacon itself is a simple iron mast that is sixty-five feet tall, at the top of which is a five-foot-long iron bar bolted at a right angle to the mast. A large iron pot filled with combustible tar hangs from the bar.

Two town guards stand by the beacon's base with a lit brazier near at hand. Should enemy ships approach by sea or troops by land, the guards will ignite the beacon. Just shy of the summit is a round watchtower, also guarded, which offers a grand vista of the town, its harbor to the east, and the surrounding lands to the north, west, and south. If a real threat to the city is detected, the guard climbs up the mast using iron bars as rungs and sets the tar on fire. As the tar ignites, flames and smoke shoot into the air and are visible for many miles on a clear day or night. When the signal is seen, each church has someone to ring the church bell alarms, and all armed Bostonians, as well as patriots living in smaller towns around the city, are expected to take up arms and hurry to the wharf area to await instructions.

meadow called the Boston Common where a few sheep and cattle continue to graze. Near the center is a small hillock topped by a stone tower and at the foot of the hill is a small shack called the Powder House.

The Boston Common, one of the city's most pastoral settings, is a beautiful, open forty-four-acre piece of gently rolling land, perfect for an afternoon of relaxation. The property was a gift in 1634 to all citizens and, by law, was designated to be commonly owned by all residents of Boston; hence its name.

City officials originally designated this parcel of open space for use as pastureland for cattle and for training the city's early militia. Today the area remains much as it was more than one hundred years ago with broad, open areas covered by grass and dirt paths that

Protesting the Stamp Act.

snake through occasional trees and wild shrubs. Most of the time, the Common is enjoyed by citizens who take pleasure in eating lunches here, letting their children run and play, and generally escaping the smell of horses and their never-ending clatter as they stumble along noisy cobblestone streets.

The Common also has a lengthy history as a place of free speech. It was here, on October 5, 1740, for example, that the evangelist George Whitefield sermonized to several thousand citizens on the importance of prayer, of examining one's hearts for spiritual guidance, and reading the bible and other good books. More recently, beginning in the early 1760s, several social groups met here to express their outrage toward the repressive actions of the hated English king. While listening to speakers, one group of radical women brought with them their spinning wheels to demonstrate the superiority of American-made clothes over those imported from England. And later, on August 14, 1765, resistance to the Stamp Act boiled over into the streets of Boston and a crowd of about one hundred marched to the Common where they hanged the effigy of the Massachusetts stamp master, Andrew Oliver, from an elm tree, verbally abused it, and set it on fire. This elm tree, known by the locals as the "Gallows Elm," is still used as one of the city's gallows. In 1660, Mary Dyer and three other Quakers were hanged from it.

As sentiment for revolution mounted and General Gage and his troops arrived to occupy Boston, many redcoats trained and camped here before they set out for

Large trees and open spaces characterize Boston Common (right), a popular place for visitors and locals to eat a quiet lunch and escape the noisy streets.

The Granary: Boston's Historic Cemetery

Located on the northwest corner of School and Tramount Streets, at the southeast corner of the Boston Common, is the burial ground known to all as the Granary. Founded in 1660, the Granary is the third oldest, yet most famous, burial ground in Boston proper. It was originally called "South Burying Ground" because at one time it was located on the most southerly area of the Boston settlement, but as Boston grew toward the south, it was later renamed "Middle Burying Ground." Its current name comes from a time when this plot of land was used as a grain storage area.

This two-acre site is a place of extraordinary beauty and history where visitors and residents alike can visit the graves of many of Boston's great patriots. Wandering through this quiet site, the curious will pass old weathered tombstones tilted forward and backward from years of harsh winters. Most of these slate tombstones are thin and rectangular with rounded tops, and they bear the name and dates of the person laid below. A few are decorated with macabre symbols such as the skull and crossbones, eerie carvings of skulls with wings, or, in places where couples are buried, two skeletons embracing each other.

Historians of the War of Independence can stand silently before the tombstones of all five bodies of the Boston patriots killed at the Boston Massacre just a few blocks from here. This is also the resting place of Peter Faneuil, founder of Faneuil Hall down near the docks; Ann Pollard, said to be the first colonist to set foot in Boston; and the parents of Benjamin Franklin. One of the more interesting graves is that of writer Elizabeth Vergoose, the prolific storyteller more commonly known as Mother Goose, who is buried with her husband and their daughter. Their epitaph reads:

> HERE LYES Ye BODY OF
> MARY GOOSE WIFE TO
> ISAAC GOOSE AGED 42
> YEARS DECD OCTOBER
> Ye 19th 1690
> Here lyes also susana
> goose ye 3 aged 13 mo
> died august ye 11th 1657

Designated as Boston's War of Independence burial ground, this resting place will eventually serve all Bostonians who played a major role in the war, including Samuel and John Adams, Paul Revere, William Dawes, and John Hancock.

Lexington and Concord on that historic day of April 18, 1775. A year later, they departed the city and never returned.

Today, the gentle slope of the Common has been returned to the citizens of the city and everyone can once again enjoy the open spaces and watch the boats moving up and down the Charles River. For a more exhilarating walk, the wharf area is the third in our tour.

The Wharf Area

To get to the wharf from the Common, take either Beacon or Common Streets east until you smell the fish and briny harbor mud that signifies Boston's wharf area. In any reasonable weather, one of the best ways to spend an aimless hour or two is to take a stroll along this enthralling wharf. Its importance to the economic life of the city is underscored by the layout of the city's wards: Nine of the twelve wards touch the wharf's shoreline and docking facilities.

The best place to experience the most colorful and historically significant wharf neighborhoods is along the Old Wharf, which is within the Great Cove on the east side. Busting at the seams, locals working and living here are weatherworn and shabbily dressed,

Shipbuilders repair an old whaler on the wharf. Touched by nine of Boston's twelve wards, the wharf area is the economic heart of the city.

A pirate approaches a young sailor. Visitors to the Old Wharf must keep an eye out for pirates, smugglers, and other criminals.

for forced labor onboard departing vessels. If you travel in groups, however, and hand out an occasional copper or two, you will not be harmed.

The most distinguishing characteristic of this area is the Long Wharf, which protrudes far out into the harbor. Completed in 1715 and at 1,586 feet, this wood pile-and-plank pier is the longest in America. To accommodate the daily loading and unloading of tons of commerce, the builders constructed the wharf 54 feet wide—30 feet of which is a roadway for handcarts and wagons while the remaining 24 feet accommodate warehouses.

A ten-minute walk both to the north and south of the Long Wharf takes ramblers to several wharves that played roles in the War of Independence. North of the Long Wharf, in ward number three, sightseers can walk to the end of Hancock's Wharf where, in 1769, the English foolishly attempted to seize John Hancock's sloop *Liberty*, an event that fanned anti-English

rubbed raw by the hard life of the sea. It is a haven for petty criminals, smugglers, pirates, and press-gangs—thugs paid to kidnap unsuspecting young men

The Charles River

Directly across from the Boston Common, the outfall of the Charles River empties into Boston Harbor. This outfall section, which is close to Boston, is heavily inundated by tidal flows that have created the hundreds of acres of salt marshes and mudflats between the town of Cambridge and Boston's west side. Although this area smells from time to time, venturing upriver a mile or so reveals some scenic and refreshing places of unrivaled beauty.

The original name for the Charles River was the Indian word *Quinobequin*, meaning "meandering." Captain John Smith, however, renamed the river after King Charles I of England to interest the king in using it as a trade route for early New Englanders. Several small brooks and streams that feed into the Charles,

Visitors who want to spend some time away from the city can go sailing on the Charles River or take a leisurely stroll along its banks.

as well as several small ponds, provide the perfect setting for a quiet stroll or picnic lunch.

Lacking the speed and force of larger rivers, the slow-moving Charles River has a brownish hue that resembles tea. This is because much of its water steeps through the abundant wetlands along its path. Swimming is still fine, however, because in spite of the color, the water is clean and refreshing.

During your short visit along the river, you may encounter one of many eight- to ten-foot-tall reddish stone dams built to cascade water over a waterwheel. These stone dams provide a wonderful splash of color in this overwhelming green landscape. The cascading water is used as a source of power to turn waterwheels that, in turn, drive machinery inside the mills that stand on the nearby riverbank. The most common mills along the Charles grind wheat into flour and cut logs into two- and four-inch-thick timbers.

Colonists dressed as Indians row out to help their fellow patriots during the Boston Tea Party. Travelers who visit Boston's wharf area can witness the site of the Tea Party and other historically significant sites.

sentiment and ignited acts of civil disobedience. South of the Long Wharf, about two hundred yards away, is Griffin's Wharf, home to the Boston Tea Party.

The day after you ramble along Tramount, the Common, and the wharf might be a good time to frequent Boston's many shops, which cater to many interests and curiosities. From the commonplace to the unusual, serious collectors and casual souvenir hunters alike will find items that are sure to please.

Chapter 6

Shopping

The shopping in Boston is the best of any major city in America. Although Boston's citizenry is still in the process of recovering from the war and a few commodities are still difficult to find, increasing French imports and production by Boston's skilled craftsmen produce sufficient items. Patriotism means buying American, so as you enjoy walking the streets, why not look for bargains.

You can purchase inexpensive everyday goods with coins, by trading with the shop owner for goods you may have with you, and by using what we call "wampum." When colonists first arrived in America, the term *wampum* referred only to the beads and shells that the Indians used as money. Today wampum includes many basic goods that one can carry in one's pockets such as tobacco, musket balls, nails, or a bottle of rum. Many colonists prefer to use the term *country money* for these items.

Quilts, silver treasures, wigs, muskets, and scrimshaw will be of interest to those desiring the city's finest and most unusual merchandise. Merchants will expect silver, or even the very rare gold coins, in exchange for these things.

Quilts

Boston is one of America's great cities for shoppers in need of high-quality quilts to keep them warm during the winter. The place to go to find some of the most imaginative designs is on Cornhill and Union Streets, down near Dock Square. The quilts sold here range in price from a quarter dollar (for simple quilts made of cotton) to as much as two dollars (for those with highly elaborate designs made of elegant silk or warm sturdy wool and linen). The stuffing inside might be taken from an old wool blanket, an older quilt, raw wool, or in some cases the stuffing is raw cotton.

A scarcity of cloth has had an influence on both the type and design of the city's unique quilts. The majority of quilt covers are made of a single piece of fabric, hence their name, whole-cloth quilts. It is also because of this scarcity that whole-cloth quilts are often made out of used and outdated quilted petticoats and other used (but still serviceable) material. Scarcity has also influenced unique quilt designs. Many of the more popular designs are made from a combination of squares and rectangles which, when sewn edge to edge, utilize every inch of material so none is wasted.

The making of quilts is often a major social activity for women. Many quilts are made at quilting bees where women and their daughters gather during the long winter months to quilt remnants together. No one wants to miss these popular social activities and the chance to catch up on local gossip. After all if you are not there, your name may be the one bandied about over the quilt frame.

Part of the reason quilts are so desirable is because of the stories they tell and scenes they depict. Whether the quilt design is stitched on the surface, a technique called appliqué, or accomplished by the combination of patches sewn together, quilt designs are unique to particular cities and towns. Favorite motifs include nature scenes such as stars, flowers and vines, feathers, and pomegranates; rural scenes

A quilter stitches a unique design. Boston quilters are well known throughout America for producing high-quality, well-crafted quilts.

such as log cabins, farmwork, and family life; and geometric designs of squares, circles, and rectangles.

Silver

Boston is awash with the shops of excellent silversmiths, also known simply as "smiths." Boston smiths are also skilled at working with gold, copper, and brass. Different silversmiths' techniques are often identical, but their work can be identified by their initials, which are stamped on each piece they make. Their initials, or some other unique mark, not only identify the makers of the pieces but also deter other smiths from forging their designs.

Be aware before contracting the work of a smith that this sort of purchase is only for the very rich. Any simple item that involves melting silver and making it into something else costs good money. Still, Boston silversmiths will never cheat you; they always use sterling silver, which is 92.5 percent silver and 7.5 percent copper. This combination of metals is necessary because pure silver is too soft to hold its form. The addition of copper strengthens it. If you wish, once you select a smith to create a fine piece, you can contribute your own silver coins or other silver items for him to melt down into memorable gifts such as dinner dishes, silverware, serving trays, cups, coffeepots, jewelry, chocolate pots, and bowls.

The city's finest smiths are considered to be sculptors, and they are among the

Pitchers and other silver pieces make beautiful but expensive souvenirs for wealthy travelers.

The process of making something out of silver is very complicated. To make a coffeepot, for instance, the smith first sketches the design, then makes a mold for the coffeepot out of graphite and hard fired clay. After the mold cools and is sanded smooth, the smith pours molten silver in between the layers of the carved mold and allows it to harden. After a final polishing, the item is ready for the purchaser. Flat pieces, such as serving trays, are crafted by first beating silver into flat sheets, then heating, shaping, and trimming those sheets to final specifications.

Wigs

As everyone new to Boston may notice, some gentlemen here wear wigs while others do not. Prior to the Revolution, when English fashion was in vogue, almost all professional men wore wigs while on the job: lawyers, doctors, educators, newspapermen, merchants, preachers, politicians, and even generals. Today, however, wigs are less in vogue, but they are still made, and many shop owners will happily help you choose the right one.

Wigs are one of many symbols that advertise a gentleman's social position and profession. Almost all professional

most respected craftspeople. Of them, the most well known are Paul Revere, Samuel Bartlett, and John Hull. Because his father was a silversmith, Revere grew up in a smith's shop. Revere's work is easily identified by his distinct designs of leaves and flowers. Some smiths double as dentists because they know how to deal with silver and gold.

The Green Dragon Tavern

Located on Union Street, just a two-block walk from Faneuil Hall, stands the venerated Green Dragon Tavern. A half-timbered, rambling, two-story establishment at the edge of the wharf, this much-loved tavern attracts a steady stream of customers. Most of the patrons are seagoing types mixed in with a smattering of merchants and gentlemen in plumed hats and velvet coats. This is a place where tourists can sit down for a bite to eat and, at the same time, experience a bit of Boston's history.

You will know that you have found the place when you see the square and compass over the front door beside a copper dragon that has turned green over the years. When entering the tavern to eat, find a table on the ground floor. The upstairs consists of a large meeting room where Boston patriots discussed the need for a revolution and strategies for fighting it. For years before the war began, the Sons of Liberty held secret sessions attended by Paul Revere, John and Samuel Adams, and John Hancock in this room. The Green Dragon was a hotbed for public political debate over a tankard of ale, and as the specter of war approached, Boston patriots

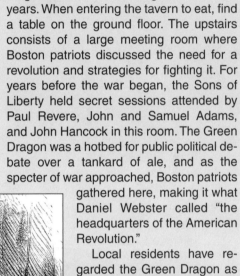

gathered here, making it what Daniel Webster called "the headquarters of the American Revolution."

Local residents have regarded the Green Dragon as a fun place to visit in the evenings for food and entertainment since it opened for business in 1657. Known for its welcoming fireplace, food, comfortable leather chairs, and friendly wagering over dart games, this is a place where guests get a feel for the pulse of the city and engage in lively political debate.

John Hancock was one of several revolutionaries who discussed strategy at the Green Dragon Tavern.

George Washington (second from left) and other members of Boston society wear traditional wigs at a ball. Today, wigs are less common but they are still fashionable and sold in shops throughout the city.

men wear them while at their jobs, and many nonprofessional men wear them in the evenings when they go out on the town. For those who have never owned a wig, a few general rules of etiquette, as well as general rules of sensibility, should be followed. One, the larger and whiter the wig, the more it costs, hence the popular term which describes such wearers as "big wigs." Be careful, however, not to overstep your social position. A man wearing a wig that is perceived to overstate his true social standing will be ridiculed by those who know him. Remember that dark wigs are generally for day use while white ones are for evenings and special occasions, and that custom-made wigs are far more expensive than common mass-produced ones.

If a gentleman desires a custom wig and is willing to spend as much as four dollars for one of the finest, his head will be shaved so a proper fitting can be made. Next, the wig maker measures the customer's head from the hairline in the front to the hairline in the back and from ear to ear. From these measurements, he makes a silk cap. The wig maker then discusses with the buyer the style, length, and composition of the finished wig. The most expensive option is human hair, followed by goat, yak, and horse. Once all the details and the price are resolved, it takes anywhere between two and three weeks for the wig maker to produce the custom wig.

During this time, the wig maker takes the silk cap, which is used as the foundation, and sets to work weaving tresses of hair into it with three to five hairs at a time. A tool called a hackle, a small wooden board that is similar to a brush and has hundreds of short nails attached to it, is used to keep the hair from tangling. It may take two to three weeks of painstaking work before the wig maker is ready to place the final touches, such as final trimming and addition of curls.

Scrimshaw

Often tourists want to return home with some work of art unique to the city and region. One of the more unusual crafts is scrimshaw, the art of carving on

An artisan carves scrimshaw into whale ivory. Such carvings provide visitors with uniquely Bostonian souvenirs.

Dangers of Whaling

The whale teeth used for the art of scrimshaw are not so easily gotten by the whalers who crack them out of the jaws of whales. Few seamen are willing to take the risks necessary to locate, harpoon, and safely return to port with the whale blubber and teeth from these leviathans.

The dangers of whaling are highlighted by the fact that whaling ships are some of the largest boats on the high seas, most between twenty and thirty tons. Yet the sperm whales they pursue can weigh three to four times as much. As whaling boats comb the coast for these prized whales, sailors climb the tallest mast to scan the horizon for the spouts that blast from whales' blowholes or the boiling sea foam that results when their huge flukes slap the water.

When a whale is sighted, two smaller rowboats are lowered, each with seven hands, six rowers, and one harpooner. Flanking both sides of the whale, the harpooners wait for the whale to break the surface before they strike. As the whale surfaces, rowers struggle to position the harpooner so he can thrust his eight-foot-long iron spear toward the heart of the whale multiple times, or if luck is with the crew, directly down the blowhole for a quick kill.

Whalers pull blubber from their catch. Whaling is dangerous because the sperm whales are such powerful and enormous creatures.

A heavy rope tied at one end to the harpoon and at the other to the rowboat prevents the harpooned whale from escaping. However, if the whale is only slightly wounded, it may dive, dragging the rowboat deep into the ocean and drowning its crew. Even more terrifying, wounded and raging whales are known to turn on the rowboats, ramming them head-on or smashing them with their powerful flukes.

whalebone and whale ivory. As is the case with all art, quality and cost vary greatly. In this case both depend on the part of the whale that is etched and the complexity of the picture.

The favorite, most sought after, and most expensive scrimshaw is etched on whale ivory, the teeth of the sperm whale, the largest of all whale species. Each adult whale has between fifty and sixty teeth along the lower jaw and each tooth is about seven inches long and weighs two pounds. The upper jaw is toothless. After the teeth are removed, some are etched by the whalers themselves, and others go to local artisans who use them to produce unique scenes.

Fine lines are etched with a thin steel tool. Whalers typically use the point of whaling knives or a sharpened sail needle, which is normally used to patch torn sails. Favored scenes for whalers depict the drama of harpooning a whale, the powerful breaching of a whale as it hurls its massive body out of the water, large sailing ships at full sail, and imaginary scenes of whales fighting giant squid. Once the scene is completed, black ink is added to the etched lines to highlight them. On board ships, whalers do not have access to the fine black inks available in Boston so they use whatever is available. Most commonly, they hand-rub the fine lines and

Handcrafted scrimshaws are lined up for sale. Skilled whalers use whatever tools and ink they have available to create these dramatic carvings on whale bone and ivory.

dots with lampblack (a black powder mixed with whale oil), squid ink, or their own tobacco "juice."

Occasionally whalers also carve the whale teeth before applying scrimshaw designs. In Boston shops, you will find carved snuffboxes, cribbage boards, portrait profiles, and a variety of knickknack items such as letter openers, candleholders, and carved figures.

The Musket Market

A musket is one item that travelers from a small city will not find at home. Complicated, slow to build, and very expensive, Boston has a small number of gunsmiths available to make them. Now that the war is over, the role of muskets has changed from using them as weapons

to using them for hunting or simply as status symbols of wealth and patriotic pride.

Because all muskets are handmade to order, no two are exactly alike and the cost is high. Men should expect to spend up to seven or eight dollars for a fair-quality musket and twice that for a beautifully decorated musket with elaborate engraving on the wood stock and iron barrel.

Although most muskets used during the war were the French Charleville and the English Land Service Musket, affectionately known here as the "Brown Bess," most for sale in Boston today are locally assembled and built for maximum accuracy. Each consists of the three familiar parts: the lock, stock, and barrel.

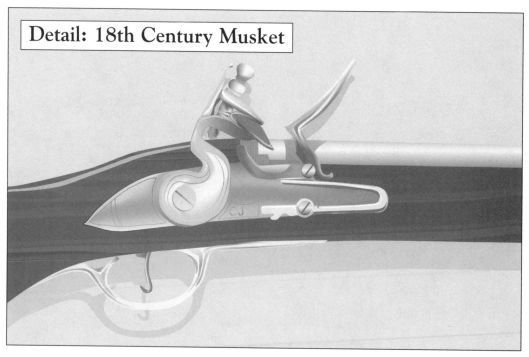

Detail: 18th Century Musket

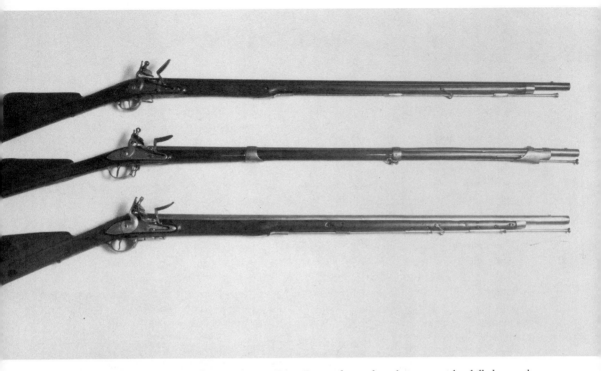

Muskets like these cannot be found in every city. Even Boston has only a few gunsmiths skilled enough to create such intricate and expensive weapons.

The lock, which is the ignition system for the musket, is a small but complex device that ignites the powder in the barrel, which in turn shoots the musket ball. Most locks are standardized, but there are choices to be made when selecting the barrel and the stock.

All barrels used in Boston muskets come from the best barrel mills in eastern Pennsylvania. They are made from solid iron bar with a smooth hole bored either one-half or three-quarter inches in diameter. A forty-five-inch barrel is standard and is reasonably accurate up to thirty feet. For large, strong men, a fifty- or even sixty-inch barrel extends accu-

racy. Bear in mind, however, that as barrel length increases, arms strain under the weight, making keen aim difficult. Although the best barrels taper in thickness toward the muzzle to reduce barrel weight, it is extremely difficult to lift a musket for more than a few seconds before fatigue sets in.

The wood stock, that part of the musket that is held firmly against the shooter's shoulder and into which the barrel screws, is hand carved to maximize comfort and accuracy. The wood used to make the stock comes directly from nearby forests. Thick planks, usually of maple, walnut, or cherry are favored. Craftsmen

How to Fire Your Musket

Firing a musket must be carefully done. If mishandled, a musket either will not fire or, worse, it may explode and injure the shooter. When properly loaded, however, the musket proves to be a highly reliable companion. Before shooting your new weapon, remember that it uses flint and powder to fire and will not operate in damp conditions. Here are the four basic steps for the proper firing of muskets:

1. Charge the musket. Place the musket on the ground with the barrel pointing up and pour powder from your powder horn down the barrel. Place a small piece of paper over the barrel, then wet a musket ball by placing it in your mouth (it must be wet to slide down the barrel), and set it on top of the paper. With your ramrod, force the wet ball and paper down the barrel on top of the powder and pack it tightly (but not too tight).

2. Bring the musket up to your shoulder and pull back the hammer (the iron piece that will snap forward and strike the flint when the trigger is pulled) to the middle position. Check the flint (the flat glasslike stone) to be sure it is properly positioned to create a spark when the iron hammer strikes it.

3. Now pour two or three pinches of powder into the small spoon-shape iron container located just below the flint (called the pan). With a dry finger, pile the powder near the tiny hole in the middle of the pan, but do not clog the hole. This tiny hole leads into the barrel where you used the ramrod to compress the powder, paper, and musket ball.

4. Pull back the hammer all the way into the rear position. Aim and pull the trigger. When the trigger is pulled, the following chain reaction occurs: The hammer flies forward, strikes the flint and creates a spark that ignites the powder in the pan. This flash of fire then travels down the tiny hole, igniting the powder that will fire the musket ball out of the barrel.

A patriot assumes the proper position and fires his musket.

use woodworking tools such as chisels, rasps, and sandpaper to create this final piece of the musket.

Many gentlemen of means enjoy highly decorative muskets suitable for Boston's annual Fourth of July parade and for display in their homes. For considerably more money, the stock and barrel makers will decorate your musket. On the stock, woodcarvers can create designs that depict battle and patriotic scenes or, more simply, the owner's name and date. The barrels can be etched with scrolling motifs or elaborate decorations of grape vines that run down the barrel.

In addition to souvenir shopping, Boston has a variety of other entertainments for the tourist. A few, such as a variety of blood sports, are recommended for men only, although women may attend. The city also has many athletic events for spectators or participants in addition to gambling games, classical music, and horse racing.

Chapter 7

Entertainment

Whether mindless entertainment or high culture is your passion, Boston appeals to the tastes of the lowbrow as well as the highbrow. Many lowbrow entertainments take place in taverns that specialize in activities such as gambling, card playing, rolling dice, cockfighting, bearbaiting, and fistfights. For highbrow guests, the city's theaters offer Shakespeare and the classical music of Europe's great composers. For those with a passion for sports, a variety of winter games are played on the ice and summer sports take place in the Common and throughout the countryside.

One of the best ways to find out about the week's entertainment is to get your hands on a copy of one of the city's two excellent newspapers: the *Boston News-Letter* and the *Gazette and Country Journal*. Both papers are four-page weeklies that print information about major events, entertainment, and goods for sale.

Not everyone who wants to read the paper needs to buy a copy—the tradition in Boston is for those who subscribe to a paper to read it, then pass it on to others who read it and, in turn, pass it on as well.

Blood Sports

Blood sports have been a favorite form of entertainment here in Boston for years. The English introduced a variety of blood sports, most popular of which are cock fighting, bearbaiting, dog fighting, and bare-knuckle boxing matches. Boston's upper class community frowns on blood sports because it views them as sordid and immoral activities, but it can do little to suppress the events since Boston's large population of roughneck sailors and wharf workers relish them.

The blood sport that attracts the most spectators is bearbaiting, featured at a handful of taverns and on occasion at the southwest corner of the Common. A bearbaiting may occur at a moment's notice, spread by word of mouth as young boys are paid to run along the wharf area and announce the contest. Sometimes the owners of bears place advertisements such as this one in the local papers:

> Bear Baiting. On Thursday next the 2nd of June, at 3 o'clock P.M., in Stratford's Street, near the Bowling Green, will be Baited a Bear, by John Coleson; where all Gentlemen and others that would divert themselves may repair.[18]

For two bits per person, crowds of both men and women, generally with cups of ale in hand, gather to watch a bear that is chained to a large stake defend itself against a pack of attacking dogs.

Each fight lasts no more than ten or fifteen minutes. The dogs never kill the bear, but they often bite it ferociously, causing it to bleed profusely. The dogs, however, do not fare as well as the bear. Although most dogs fight many times, others die from the loss of a leg or from a quick swipe of the bear's claws, a blow that rips the poor animal open and sends it flying into the crowd. Whatever the outcome, the owner of the bear does not want the bear killed. Although bears live in the forests

Bare-knuckle boxing matches like this one have been popular in Boston for decades. Boxing and other blood sports are common entertainment for the city's working class.

outside of Boston, they are difficult to find and even more difficult to tame and train.

If the sight of blood is not to your liking, perhaps you will better enjoy watching some athletic games where people compete with each other.

Athletic Events

Many athletic contests are played on Sunday afternoons throughout the city. Anyone wishing to play or simply sit and watch should wander over to the Common or to Jamaica Pond, a few miles south of the city, on a sunny afternoon.

One of the favorite games played on the Common is called whiffle. This sport, which requires nine players on each side, involves a soft ball the size of a fist, a stick, and four bases placed in a square about fifty feet apart. The object of whiffle is for a player standing at one base to hit the ball with a stick as far away from opposing players as possible. Then that player runs to any one of the other three bases trying to avoid being hit by the ball thrown at him by one of the opposing players.

Another favorite sport that involves running is a game called football. In this

 Cockfighting

One of the more brutal blood sports favored by a large segment of Boston's population is cockfighting. These contests are found at about a dozen Boston taverns that are fitted with arenas where cheering spectators can wager money on the outcome of the contest. Cockfighting is a contest in which two roosters are placed in a pit to fight—usually to the death. To speed the outcome of the fight, the back of the feet of each bird, called the spurs, are fitted with sharp steel blades that are one to three inches long.

A few minutes before each fight, bettors may inspect the birds and handle them to test their weight, feel their muscles, and get the sense of the birds' enthusiasm for the fight. Then the owners of the cocks bring them into the arena, a circular pit no larger than ten feet in diameter with a four-foot-high perimeter wall around which the spectators sit on wood bleachers. While awaiting the start, tavern owners sell beer and a variety of foods.

The owners enter the arena, holding the birds in front of each other at its center. Enthusiasm for the upcoming fight is piqued as the birds peck at each other's faces. This initial sparring brings cheers from the crowd. Then, when the tavern owner signals, the owners release the cocks to attack. At that moment the birds hurl themselves upon each other, beak against beak and breast to breast, while their steel spurs furiously cut into flesh in the hope of making a fatal slash that will end the contest. Following several attacks, the center of the arena is littered with feathers and spots of dirt moistened by blood.

After no more than ten minutes, one of the cocks falters and falls to the ground. The fight is over, the winner declared by the tavern owner, losing bettors pay up, winners are paid off, and the birds are carried out by their owners. Although the contest ends when only one cock remains standing, often both will hemorrhage to death.

A crowd gathers to watch a cockfight. One of Boston's most brutal blood sports, cockfighting pits two roosters against each other in a fight to the death.

game, two teams of several players try to kick a ball (no hands allowed) across the other team's goal line. The first to do so successfully wins the game. The rules are somewhat unclear, but the game resembles the sprawling and brawling game played during the Shrovetide festival popular in England. It is played here primarily by Harvard students, but citizens willing to risk the loss of a tooth or a bloody nose are welcome to give it a try.

A third, but far more civilized, sporting favorite enjoyed by more genteel citizens is foot racing. Many foot races are held throughout the city: the Beacon Hill race, in which contestants run from the top to the bottom of Beacon Hill; the Commons race, around the perimeter of the Common; the Long Wharf run, to the end of

Winter Outdoor Activities

Summer is not the only time for fun in Boston. Although Bostonians have several months of cold weather and snow, citizens get outside and enjoy themselves even in severe winter weather. The best places to go depend upon whether your favorite activity is sledding, ice skating, ice hockey, or sleigh riding.

Sledding is especially popular with schoolchildren, and the favorite place to sled is on School Street right outside of the Boston Latin School. From the front steps of the school, the slope of the street is perfect for sledding down one of several hills. Sledding down to Cornhill Street was a tradition long before the war, but it is even more so now because when the English occupied Boston, one of the governors who lived on School Street tossed ashes from his fireplace onto the sled run to stop the boys from sledding. The complaint by the boys was so strident that the governor ceased his attempt to stop the sledding.

For those who enjoy both skating and hockey, the place to go when the temperature plummets is to either side of the Neck where the shallow water freezes before the deeper water in the main harbor. Here, you will find Bostonians skating on boots that blacksmiths have fitted with iron blades (the blades have been nailed to the bottoms of the boots). Young boys enjoy playing the game of ice hockey, which the English introduced prior to the Revolution. This is a game of two teams, sometimes as many as one hundred on a side, who use wood sticks to knock a round ball into the opposing team's red net. The opposing team, of course, tries to prevent the ball from going in. The games are always played in one of the many small coves found on Shawmut to isolate the many players from casual ice skaters because the game can, and frequently does, turn aggressive.

the wharf and back; and the longest of them all, the marathon from the fortifications at the Neck in the South End to Hunt's Wharf in the North End.

Horse Racing

At an early date in Boston's history, horses became a prime commodity of trade from the West Indies. Initially horses were worked on farms and used as transportation, but young men eager to match their steeds against those of their friends quickly made them into prized race horses. Bostonians' interest in speed and wagering soon found an outlet. Initially, the selectmen were angered by racing and outlawed the sport within four miles of the city, citing it as a corrupting influence.

Public opinion, however, eventually superseded law. Check the *Boston Newsletter* for races run in Cambridge, at Rumley Marsh, and between Menotomy and Cambridge. Most races are run across open meadows and fields, sometimes across shallow streams, and occasionally over low walls and fences. Each race begins at one town or tavern and ends at another. Most races are one direction, and advertisements in the newspapers always stipulate the prize money that goes to the winner. Pick up a newspaper and join other race fans at the starting point.

Spectators have the option of standing to the sides of the race route and awaiting the charging horde of horses to thunder by, or following behind the race horses on their own horses. The number of entries is usually limited to thirty horses. The larger horses are required to carry additional weight in the form of stone-filled saddlebags to give smaller horses a fair chance at winning. Wagering

among spectators is popular and the winners and losers are mostly good-natured about their fortunes.

The Concert Hall

For those seeking fine music, Boston's Concert Hall is the place to hear American music as well as the music of some of Europe's great composers. Tickets are sold by subscription only so interested visitors will need to ask Bostonians for extra tickets. Each concert in the series, which often includes both music and singing, typically plays at the Concert

Horses and their riders battle for first place in a race. Excited by the high-speed challenge and the opportunity to gamble, Bostonians host many horse races throughout the year.

A Traditional Thanksgiving Dinner

The traditional Thanksgiving feast, also called the Harvest Festival by many Bostonians, remains a time-honored tradition for gathering families. Even among the well-to-do, the Thanksgiving feast is kept relatively modest in honor of the simplicity of the first Thanksgiving celebrated by our Puritan ancestors.

According to custom, the feast begins with a Protestant prayer before the dishes are brought to the table. Typical fare features roasted fowl on a platter (generally goose, swan, or turkey) with onions arranged around the bottom of the platter. Secondary traditional foods include Indian cornbread, standing dish of pompions (cooked pumpkin, cinnamon, butter, and brown sugar), boiled sallet (boiled cabbage, currants, sugar, butter, and vinegar), frumenty (an Indian wheat pudding made of hulled wheat boiled in milk, with sugar plums), and perhaps a dessert of prune tarts or pumpkin pudding.

Dishes are placed on the table and guests serve and carve for themselves. Although imported from England, a small number of people use forks, but eating utensils at a traditional Thanksgiving feast are limited to a knife and a spoon that diners bring from home. Napkins are used not only to clean one's mouth and fingers, but also to pick up hot morsels of food or to hold a bird for carving. Each guest takes the food they wish to eat from each serving dish and either eats it immediately or places it on a thick piece of bread, called a trencher, that functions as a plate. At the end of the meal, the trencher may be eaten.

Early Puritan settlers celebrate the first Thanksgiving. This feast remains an annual tradition for many Bostonian families.

Hall once a week but will remain in the city for six to eight weeks to give all interested an opportunity to attend. The cost of each ticket, a half dollar for each performance, is sufficiently steep to exclude all but the most refined and well-heeled ladies and gentlemen. All concerts begin at 6:30 P.M. sharp.

By far, the most popular concerts are quartets and accompanying soloists. Favorite instruments include the violin and its larger cousin the viola de gamba, harpsichord, hautboy (sometimes called an oboe), and French horn. On occasion, when Bostonians wish to enjoy an evening of Bach or Buxtehude organ music, especially some of the favored fugues, all gather in the King's Chapel of the Anglican Church to listen to the organ donated by Thomas Brattle. The occasional military band provides further variety when patriotic events are celebrated. Very often at the end of a concert, all attendees roll up their sleeves and lend a hand in removing all chairs to clear space for a grand dance before adjourning for the evening.

The favorite composer in Boston today is clearly the German-born George Frideric Handel, who lived much of his adult life in London. His most-often performed composition is the *Messiah*. One reason for its popularity is that many Boston families are invited to sing the choral sections for each of the performances. In addition to Handel and Bach, other favorite composers in Boston include the Italian composers Vivaldi and Corelli.

Chapter 8

Day Trips
Outside Boston

Boston is the commercial, cultural, and economic heart of Massachusetts, and because of this, it sometimes overshadows neighboring towns that also have much to offer. Many local towns, although small, have left their own unique stamp on American history and offer cultural attractions worth exploring. For those with the time and interest to experience these cultural and historical treasures, four gems await you: Cambridge, Concord, Salem, and Nantucket Island. Each of these places has its own lifestyle and offers visitors sights and experiences that cannot be found in the more noisy, more expensive, and definitely more crowded Boston.

Boston is linked to these four locales by a system of commercial stagecoaches that travel on a daily schedule. Schedules and fares are posted at the way station near Faneuil Hall. Simply show up on time and purchase your ticket. The closest of the four is the picturesque aca-

demic town of Cambridge, which lies immediately west a few miles up the Charles River.

Cambridge

From downtown Boston, just four miles up the Charles River, vacationers can take an eight-mile stagecoach ride across the Neck or a more pleasant and quicker ferryboat ride from the west side dock to Cambridge. For five pennies each direction, the ferryboat ride lasts just thirty minutes or so, depending upon the river's current and the number of available rowers. As you board the ferry, notice the wood bridge being constructed across the Back Bay from Boston's west side to Cambridge. It is nearly finished and will provide Boston with its first bridge across the bay.

As you disembark, take Water Street directly into Cambridge, a town of enormous historic value, which was originally called Newtowne until 1638 when it was renamed after Cambridge, England. As you walk north on Water Street, you will pass the center of town where families built their homes. Farm fields lay just outside of the town. A left turn on Cambridge Street leads to the Cambridge Common, owned by locals, where cows graze. The large elm on the northwest corner of the Common is the very place where General Washington mustered his troops prior to marching into Boston a few days before the Battle of Bunker Hill.

As its greatest claim to fame, the town has the honor of having been General

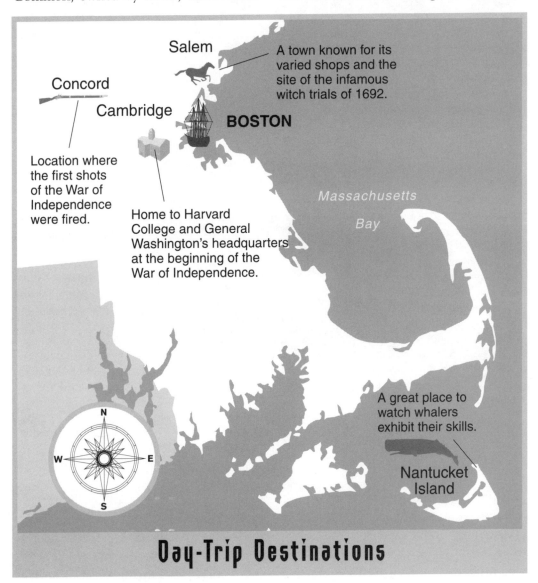

Salem
A town known for its varied shops and the site of the infamous witch trials of 1692.

Concord

Cambridge

BOSTON

Location where the first shots of the War of Independence were fired.

Home to Harvard College and General Washington's headquarters at the beginning of the War of Independence.

Massachusetts Bay

A great place to watch whalers exhibit their skills.

Nantucket Island

N
W E
S

Day-Trip Destinations

Flour Mills

The flour mills found in Cambridge and other neighboring towns are both picturesque and fascinating. From a distance, flour mills that process flour by water cascading over a large wooden wheel are a captivating and soothing sight in the countryside. They are also worth entering to study close-up the fascinating engineering required to grind grain into flour. Visitors will marvel at the mechanical precision with which a flour mill operates.

Inside the mill, visiting tourists will hear the creaking of the waterwheel and the many wooden gears that transmit the power of the spinning waterwheel to the two flat millstones that grind the grain inside. The twin identically matched circular stones are anywhere between four and six feet in diameter and three feet thick. The stones are always manufactured to be precisely the same size and made from the same type of hard stone, usually granite. The two stones are positioned flat at the mill, one directly on top of the other with a tiny clearance in between them. The grinding surface of each stone has hundreds of small grooves that are about an eighth inch deep and radiate from the center to the edge. These grooves channel out the flour, spilling it over the edge as the wheels spin.

As the stones spin at about fifty revolutions per minute, the miller pours the grain down a tube to the center of the two stones, and the seeds tumble out in between the two grinding surfaces. As the millstones pulverize the grain, the flour that spills onto the floor is shoveled into bags for the customer.

The skill of a good miller is in his ability to carefully adjust the space between the two stones. Each type of grain is different in size, and the miller needs to be certain that the space is small enough to thoroughly crush the small seeds— about the thickness of a piece of cardboard for wheat —but not too small because the spinning granite stones might touch and thereby create enough friction to burn the wheat. To ensure that the stones are not touching, the miller keeps his nose close to the grindstone to detect the smell of burning grain.

Washington's headquarters during the opening salvos of the war. The Common billeted most of Washington's twenty-thousand-man army, and the rest occupied private homes, Christ Church, and buildings at Harvard College. When you wander back to the ferry at the end of the day, you will get a personal feel for the war by exploring some of the earth works or dirt for fortifications, that face

Boston across the river, behind which our troops spied on the redcoats in Boston. And if time permits, even older earth works, called the "pallysadoe," can still be found. They are stockade fences and trenches built more than one hundred years ago by the early Puritans to keep the Indians at a distance.

For the moment, however, let us wander over to Harvard College, the present-day focus of activities in Cambridge. To get there, backtrack five blocks east on Cambridge Street. The college was founded by the General Council of Massachusetts in 1636 to train young men for the ministry and for positions of leadership within the religious community. It was not until two years after the college was founded that it was named after a young pastor from nearby Charles Town who bequeathed his library of 329 books and half of his estate to the fledgling school. That young pastor was John Harvard. Although some of the initial money for the college came from public money, attendance is still very expensive; tuition for one year for a young man from a

middle-class family is equal to one to two years of his father's income.

To visit the college, walk down Braintree or Kirkland Streets, which run right through the campus. Although enrollment has declined because of the war, there is still a full-time faculty of nine professors and a library of five thousand books. A walk about the campus is a pleasant way to spend an hour observing the six major buildings as well as an additional six or seven private nearby homes that will soon be converted into additional classrooms. The six buildings seen today, all of which are between three and five stories tall, make up the present campus, but plans for expansion are underway as more and more students and faculty return.

The brick stairs of Harvard Hall are dimpled, thanks to students who drop cannon balls on them from upper-story rooms. The cannon balls are heated outside the hall in fires and quickly carried to

Harvard College, as it looked in 1720.

Freshman Life at Harvard

Harvard experienced a decline in enrollment during the war. Newly enrolled students have brought the freshman class back to its usual number of seventy-five young men. Of this number, an occasional scholarship is available for the poor. Other poor cover part of their tuition with farm produce bartered in exchange for instruction. The vast majority of freshmen, however, are the sons of wealthy landowners and successful merchants.

Because of the disparity in income between the very rich and the very poor, a blatant form of class ranking takes place and can make freshman life here pleasant or depressingly unpleasant. On each student's first day on campus, the college steward publicly ranks each young man according to what is called his "supposed family dignity," or family wealth, and every freshman knows how close to the top or to the bottom he stands. This social ranking determines such things as a student's order of recitation in class, where each sits at evening meal, the order in which he is served, where students march in academic processionals, and the location of their names in the annual college catalog.

All freshmen, regardless of social standing, are subjected to hazing. Upperclassmen may make freshmen run errands, share their food, sing demeaning songs, or run naked in the snow past the president's residence. No freshman is allowed to wear a hat in Harvard Yard unless it is raining or snowing, and he is walking with his hands full of books. Freshmen are not allowed to socialize with older students and are to step off sidewalks to make way for approaching upperclassmen. In spite of many insulting taunts, freshmen do not give up and go home, because they would rather be at Harvard than following behind a plow or working in their fathers' businesses.

their rooms during the winter as a source of heat, then simply tossed out the window to be reheated the next night. Between Harvard Hall and Holden Chapel is Hollis Hall, where students claim bragging rights to the nearby "Rebellious Elm." It earned that name in 1768 when rebellious students met there to pledge not to drink English tea, and again on April 19, 1775, when a few Harvard students used it as a gathering place before setting out to defend Concord's North Bridge at the outbreak of the war.

Concord

Twenty miles due west from Boston is Concord, one of Massachusetts's most beautiful and most historically significant small towns. The primary reason people visit Concord is to see and experience the place where the first shots rang out at the start of the War of Independence. The one must-see here is the North Bridge, the place where the minutemen took their stand against the redcoats. The North Bridge that spans the Concord River is found north of Concord, a quarter of a mile on the Lowell Road that leads to the city of Lowell.

The bridge that arches across the river today is the same one where minutemen fired shots in April 19, 1775, to block the English advance. As you approach it, you will see the six sets of pilings that support the elegant arching bridge, the railings on both sides, and the loose oak plank surface, which wagon drivers and walkers rearrange as necessary. It was these planks that the British soldiers attempted to remove in order to prevent the minutemen from crossing during their historic encounter. As most will recognize, the bridge, just eighteen feet wide and eighty feet long, is in terrible condition and the Concord city council plans to tear it down at the end of the year.

With a good part of the day left for exploring picturesque Concord, why not head just two miles south of the city on South Road to visit beautiful Walden Pond. A favorite retreat for the local inhabitants for many years, Walden Pond has been a haven at which people fish, hunt, and paddle birch-bark canoes.

Autumn trees frame Walden Pond. An oasis just south of Concord, Walden Pond provides visitors with a beautiful place to enjoy a variety of outdoor activities.

Fishermen come here to catch rainbow trout, freshwater perch, and smallmouth bass, while hunters favor gray squirrels, chipmunks, rabbits, raccoons, and red foxes. These small animals are difficult to kill with muskets, so most hunters use snares and bows and arrows. The bow and arrow is preferred because it is quiet and because missed shots can be retrieved and used again. The pond is also a favorite habitat for birds such as kingfishers, blackbirds, red-tailed hawks, and chickadees, and in the spring and fall, migratory ducks and geese pass overhead and land in nearby marshes for food and rest.

For a change of geography, travel north of Boston along the coast to the small town of Salem, one of the area's most scenic fishing villages.

Salem

An easy one day's journey by carriage, wagon, or horse, the small, picturesque seaport town of Salem lies just twenty miles north of Boston. In many respects, Salem is a miniature Boston complete with sailing ships that dot the harbor and wharves alive with the activities of loading and unloading ships. One local resident describes Salem this way, "Seemingly, the wealth of the world is

The historic town of Salem is an easy one-day excursion twenty miles north of Boston.

Salem fishermen net a bounty of seafood that will end up at some of the town's finest markets and taverns.

funneled into Salem, great houses, silk gowns, pianos, French perfume, carriages, and carriage horses."[19] Contrary to such elegance, the occasional pirate ship still occasionally harasses ships headed north toward Nova Scotia. When pirate ships are spotted, the city's great bell is furiously rung, warning ships in the harbor to either remain in harbor or to group together before venturing forth into the open seas.

Although Salem's population is considerably smaller than Boston's, it is still the sixth largest city in America, a tribute to its successful harbor, shipbuilding facilities, and fishing grounds which teem with a variety of large fish. As many locals will tell you, Salem's codfish trade with the West Indies and Europe is what drew early colonists here in the first place, more than 150 years ago. It is this prosperity that accounts for the many elegant homes (built by Salem merchants) that grace the low hills up from the docks. For anyone who has an interest in architecture and elegant liv-

ing, a walk along Essex and Winthrop Streets is a necessity. Salem architect and wood-carver Samuel McIntire is responsible for many of the stunning architectural treasures found here.

War historians will appreciate Salem, which like Boston, played a significant role in the war. In 1774 a provincial congress was organized in Salem and the political revolution began. Two months before the battles in Lexington and

Concord, skirmishes broke out in Salem. And once the war broke out, Salem's fleet contributed mightily to the war effort, capturing or sinking 455 English vessels.

Residents of Salem are proud of their heritage, with the exception of one event that occurred almost one hundred years ago and has done more to tarnish the city's reputation than its many positive contributions. In January 1692 when two young children fell ill and the doctor could not heal them, he declared that they had been bewitched. This reckless diagnosis began the city's darkest year, which culminated with the lynching of nineteen men and women, all of whom were accused of practicing witchcraft.

These poor souls and another hundred, who were eventually released from prison, were accused without evidence of having caused the death of citizens by casting spells on them. When children died of smallpox or a tribe of Indians attacked the

city, fearful, ignorant citizens cried out the names of their enemies, declaring them witches. In June 1692 the trials began and the guilty were hung at the city's gallows, which are still standing today. For those interested in the macabre, the hill where the gallows once stood is found at the west end of town near Boston Street. Although the infamous courthouse was torn down in 1760, it stood at the present-day intersection of Washington and Lynde Streets.

Giles Corey, a resident of Salem, stands accused of witchcraft in a Salem courtroom.

Nantucket Island

Thirty miles off the south coast of Cape Cod is the Gray Lady of the Sea. Welcome to the island of Nantucket, dubbed the "Gray Lady" by whalers because of the thick fog that sweeps across the island without warning. Getting there costs most visitors four hours of their time onboard a ferry that travels back and forth between the island and Cape Cod. The journey can be daunting—the deep rolling swells that can on occasion swallow ships are not for the faint-hearted or the weak-stomached.

In addition to the island's peaceful existence, its biggest attraction is the chance to see the whalers at work. This old profession, first learned from the Indians, employs one-third of the island's population. One hundred fifty whaling ships roam the Atlantic Ocean from Greenland as far south as Brazil.

Few inns dot the island, but many homeowners rent out rooms to whalers waiting for their boats to depart. If the boats are out to sea, make your visit here more enjoyable by staying with families that rent rooms. You will not need to walk the island looking for them because the children of these families await the arrival of ferry boats from the Cape. They greet suitcase-toting tourists with a smile and help those tourists with their belongings if they agree to follow them to their homes.

An interesting feature of some Cape houses is the graceful bow roof, slightly curved like the bottom of a boat and covered with fog-gray shingles. Also unique to these houses is an abundance of small, irregularly shaped and located windows in the gable ends. The gardens of these homes are regularly swept by salty sea breezes yet manage to give life to a profusion of sweet-scented bayberry most of the year, and wild roses and daffodils in late spring and early summer. The cobblestones that pave many Nantucket streets are also used as ballast on the empty returning ships that deliver whale oil to England.

In 1659 a group of nine Massachusetts Englishmen purchased the island from the Wampanoag for about one hundred dollars and two beaver hats. The English then raised sheep but shortly learned from the Indians how to strip and process blubber from whales that became stranded on the beaches. The processed blubber produced low-grade oil suitable for sale as a fuel for lamps. This new source of income motivated the English to catch more whales.

In search of an additional source of revenue, in 1672 the islanders sought whaling captains and their boats to settle on the island and to hunt the whales that annually migrate past the island. Following many slow years during the War of Independence, Nantucket has now regained its title as "Whaling Capital of the World" and has become one of the largest cities in Massachusetts.

Whalers boil down blubber for oil on a ship off Nantucket Island, the "Whaling Capital of the World."

The wharf where whales are hauled out for processing has everyone holding their noses. Leviathans harpooned near the island are secured to the sides of ships with ropes and winched up wooden skids into enormous warehouses where visitors can watch the rending process. First, carvers wielding curved knives attached to long wood handles slice the blubber into chunks that are then slid into huge iron caldrons encased in brick called try-works,

or more commonly, blubber pots. There, fires reduce the blubber to oil, which is used for candles and lamps.

In addition to the sights, sounds, and smells of the wharf, the island offers other unique sights as well. A walk to Brant Point Lighthouse, at the north end of the island, features the oldest lighthouse in America. It was built in 1746 to guard the harbor's northern entrance.

Notes

Introduction: Freedom's Birthplace

1. Richard Baxter, *Baxter's Practical Works, Vol. 4, The Reformed Pastor.* Morgan, PA: Soli Deo Gloria, 1992, p. 227.
2. Quoted in Joe McCarthy, *New England.* New York: Time, 1967, p. 62.

Chapter One: A City on a Hill: A Brief History of Boston

3. Quoted in Andrew Buni and Alan Rogers, *Boston, a City on a Hill.* Woodland Hills, CA: Windsor, 1984, p. 14.
4. Quoted in Thomas H. O'Connor, *The Hub: Boston Past and Present.* Boston: Northeastern University Press, 2001, p. 18.
5. Quoted in Buni and Rogers, *Boston,* p. 37.
6. Quoted in Buni and Rogers, *Boston,* p. 41.
7. Quoted in William F. Robinson, *Coastal New England.* Boston: New York Geographic Society, 1983, pp. 82–83.

Chapter Two: Arrival, Weather, and Location

8. Quoted in Robinson, *Coastal New England,* p. 67.

9. Quoted in "On the Road: Modes of Travel in the New Republic," *American Studies at The University of Virginia,* 2002. www.xroads.virginia. edu.
10. Carl Seaburg, *Boston Observed.* Boston: Beacon Press, 1971, p. 156.

Chapter Three: First Day: Getting Around, Where to Stay, What to Eat

11. Quoted in Buni and Rogers, *Boston,* p. 15.
12. William G. Hill, "An Early Biographical Sketch of Deacon Edward Convers," *Roots Web,* 2003. www. rootsweb. com.
13. Quoted in Jessica Kross, *American Eras: The Colonial Era 1600–1754.* Detroit: Gayle Information, 1998, p. 292.

Chapter Four: Four Historic Landmarks

14. Quoted in Robinson, *Coastal New England,* p. 123.
15. "A Student's History of American Literature," *Bootlegged Books,* 2003. www.bootleggedbooks.com.
16. Quoted in "Boston Tea Party Gazette," *Boston Tea Party Ship and Museum,* 2000. www.bostonteaparty ship.com.

Chapter Five: Three Casual Walks

17. Quoted in Marilynn Johnson, "Beacon Hill," *Emerson College*, 2003. www.emerson.edu.

Chapter Seven: Entertainment

18. Quoted in George Francis Dow, *Every Day Life in the Massachusetts Bay Colony.* New York: Dover, 1988, p. 114.

Chapter Eight: Day Trips Outside Boston

19. Robinson, *Coastal New England*, p. 90.

For Further Reading

Jane Holtz Kay, *Preserving New England*. New York: Pantheon, 1986. This beautifully written book, filled with photographs of New England, focuses on the many historic sites worthy of preservation. One chapter focuses on Massachusetts and the legacy of Boston during the colonial period and subsequent revolution. The book also provides an excellent early history of Boston.

Harold and James Kirker, *Bulfinches' Boston*. New York: Oxford University Press, 1964. This work describes the great buildings and architecture of the late eighteenth and early nineteenth centuries. The focus of the book is on the architectural influence of Charles Bulfinch (1763–1844), who is still regarded as Boston's greatest architect.

Peter R. Knights, *Yankee Destinies: The Lives of Ordinary Nineteenth Century Bostonians*. Chapel Hill: University of North Carolina Press, 1991. The author provides lively discussions about life in late-eighteenth and nineteenth-century Boston. Topics include marriage and raising children, working in the city, the commerce of the city, and the everyday perils and pleasures of living in a large city.

Joe McCarthy, *New England*. New York: Time, 1967. This book is part of the Time-Life Library of America and as such provides an excellent overview of the history and culture of New England. Several sections in the book focus on Boston and its central role in colonial America.

James Schouler, *Americans of 1776*. New York: Dodd, Mead, 1906. James Schouler's work is an excellent study of life in colonial America. Using newspapers, magazines, and diaries, he presents a broad spectrum of information on topics of dress, pastimes, fashion, family homes, home life, literature, the colonial press, religion, music, theater, and etiquette.

Works Consulted

Books

Richard Baxter, *Baxter's Practical Works, Vol. 4, The Reformed Pastor.* Morgan, PA: Soil Deo Gloria, 1992. This volume contains Baxter's important speech, "Compassionate Counsel to all Young Men," which he wrote and delivered in 1681.

Andrew Buni and Alan Rogers, *Boston, a City on a Hill.* Woodland Hills, CA: Windsor, 1984. This book covers the history of Boston from the arrival of the Algonquian through 1984. The first four chapters focus on colonial Boston and are complemented by maps, paintings, and original documentation.

George Francis Dow, *Every Day Life in the Massachusetts Bay Colony.* New York: Dover, 1988. The author attempts to recreate life in colonial America by providing information and descriptions of everything from Boston's architecture and street construction to the manners and meals enjoyed by Bostonians. Containing anecdotes, documents, and descriptions of actual events, this book is a treasury of information for all students studying the American Revolution.

Jessica Kross, *American Eras: The Colonial Era 1600–1754.* Detroit: Gayle Information, 1998. This is the second volume in an American history series. Following an introductory chapter about the colonial era, the book covers dozens of topics such as the arts, business and communications, the people of colonial America, education, government and politics, law and justice, lifestyles, and social trends.

Thomas H. O'Connor, *The Hub: Boston Past and Present.* Boston: Northeastern University Press, 2001. Professor O'Connor chronicles the events that shaped Boston's distinctive character over the centuries, beginning with the city's origin in the Puritan settlement on the Shawmut Peninsula. He then traces its expansion as a leading port and commercial center, and highlights its importance in the struggle for American independence.

William F. Robinson, *Coastal New England*. Boston: New York Geographic Society, 1983. This book provides an excellent combination of text and photographs that gives a clear and complete history of the town and city life along the New England coast. The author focuses much of the book on Boston in the past three centuries.

Carl Seaburg, *Boston Observed*. Boston: Beacon Press, 1971. Seaburg's book covers the span of Boston's history from its start to the year 1970. The primary focus, however, is on the early years up to the Revolutionary War. Using the quotations of many early Bostonians, the author supports his conclusion that the wharves of Boston were the economic, spiritual, and cultural backbone of the city.

Walter Muir Whitehall, *Boston: A Topographical History*. Cambridge, MA: Harvard University Press, 1968. The author presents a thorough discussion of the topography of Boston as it changed and influenced the architectural development of the city from the eighteenth century to 1968.

Periodical
Boston News-Letter, November 26, 1741.

Internet Sources
"Boston Tea Party Gazette," *Boston Tea Party Ship and Museum*, 2000. www.bostonteapartyship.com.

R. J. Brown, "First American Newspapers," *The History Buff*, 2003. www.historybuff. com.

"The Granary Burying Ground," http://med-pharm53.bu.edu.

Paul Hashagen, "Taking Charge: The Evolution of Fireground Command," *The American Fire Service*, 2002. www.firehouse.com.

William G. Hill, "An Early Biographical Sketch of Deacon Edward Convers," *Roots Web*, 2003. www.rootsweb.com.

"History of Boston Latin School," *Boston Latin School*, 2002. www.bls.org.

Marilynn Johnson, "Beacon Hill," *Emerson College*, 2003. www.emerson.edu.

"On the Road: Modes of Travel in the New Republic," *American Studies at The University of Virginia*, 2002. www.xroads.virginia.edu.

"Passage to America, 1750," *Eye Witness: History Through the Eyes of Those Who Lived It*. www.ibiscom.com.

"A Student's History of American Literature," *Bootlegged Books*, 2003. www.bootleggedbooks.com.

Peggy Tebbetts, "Copp's Hill Burial Ground," 2002. www.geocities.com.

Websites

The Avalon Project at Yale Law School (www.yale.edu). This website provides an outstanding collection of documents for American law, history, and diplomacy from the eighteenth to the twenty-first centuries.

The Boston Historical Society (www.bostonhistory.org). The Boston Historical Society is a growing organization which operates several of the city's oldest historical sites. Their website provides excellent and accurate information about many of the city's oldest sites.

Rutgers University (www.newark.rutgers.edu). Rutgers University's "Eighteenth-Century Resources" website provides an excellent array of documentation on the American Revolution. This link is rich with colonial speeches, laws, and journals that illustrate and describe Boston's colonial period.

Index

Picture Credits

About the Author

James Barter received his undergraduate degree in history and classics at the University of California at Berkeley, followed by graduate studies in ancient history and archaeology at the University of Pennsylvania. Barter has taught history as well as Latin and Greek.

A Fulbright scholar at the American Academy in Rome, Barter worked on archaeological sites in and around the city as well as on sites in the Naples area. He also has worked and traveled extensively in Greece.

Barter currently lives in Rancho Santa Fe, California, with his seventeen-year-old daughter Kalista.